In Love with Paris

Artwork by Gérard Ramon

Betimes Books

First published in the English language in 2016 by Betimes Books, Paris, France

www.betimesbooks.com

ISBN 978-2-7466-8421-8

Cover design by JT Lindroos

Contents

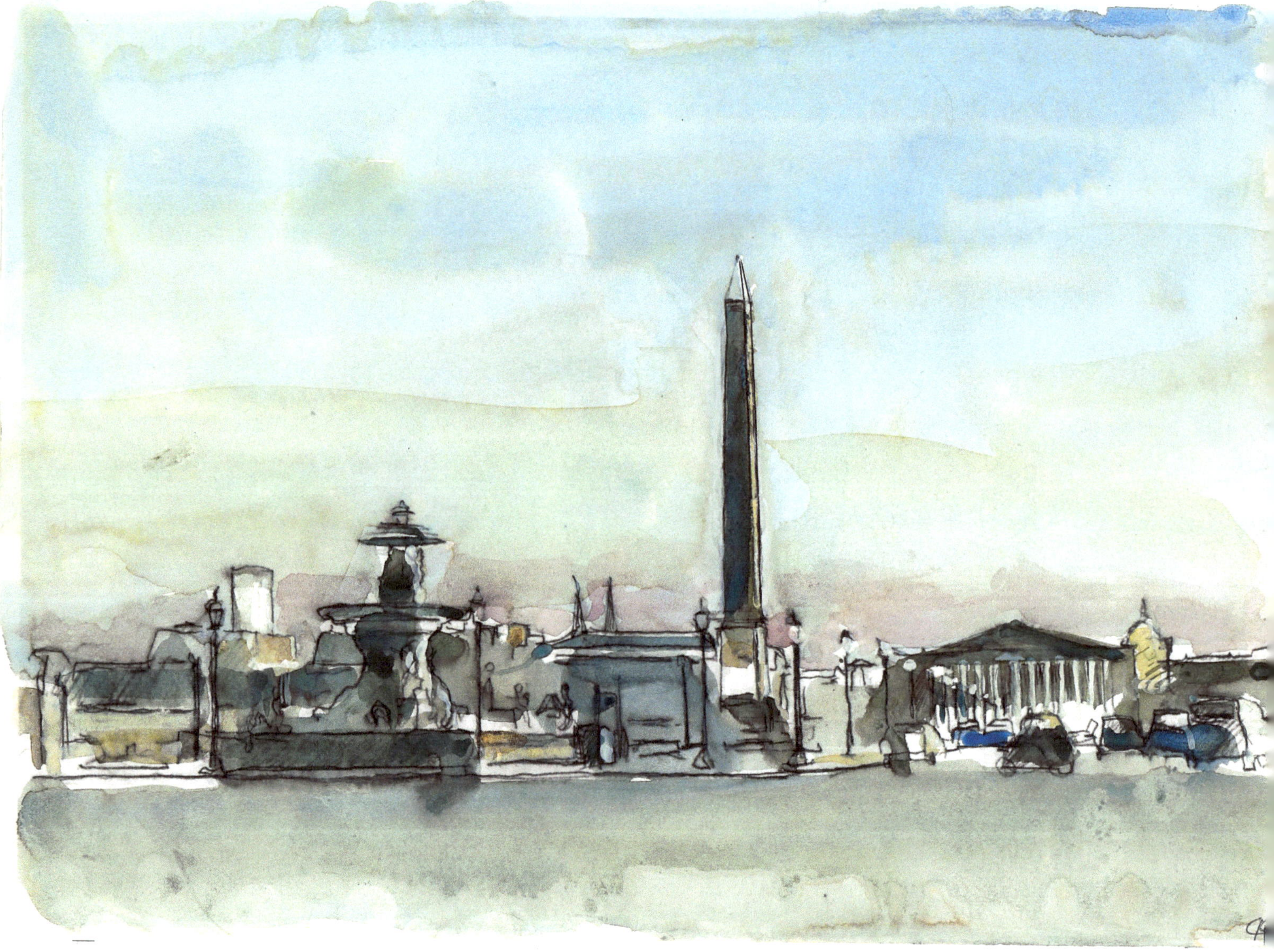

An artist's stroll around Paris

I'm lucky enough to be born and living all my life in Paris and so I've undertaken the arduous task of a graphic description of my city. Walking in the streets of Paris with a sketch book and a few pencils, taking in the air of the city, stopping to do a quick drawing or a watercolour... Isn't it a dream for many artists? The atmosphere of Paris is so indefinable, its light so translucent; every street, every square a witness of its rich past and yet so modern and so full of life.

With my drawings, I would like to invite you to walk with me along the river, to stride across its bridges, to sit on a terrace of a Paris bistro and watch the world walk by, to discover or rediscover the city through the eyes of a Parisian.

I tried to capture this mysterious "air de Paris", this "je ne sais quoi" that makes Paris so different from any other city in the world. I didn't think it possible, but with every new drawing, I was falling deeper and deeper in love with her, and I hope that you will, too.

Gérard Ramon, Paris, 2016

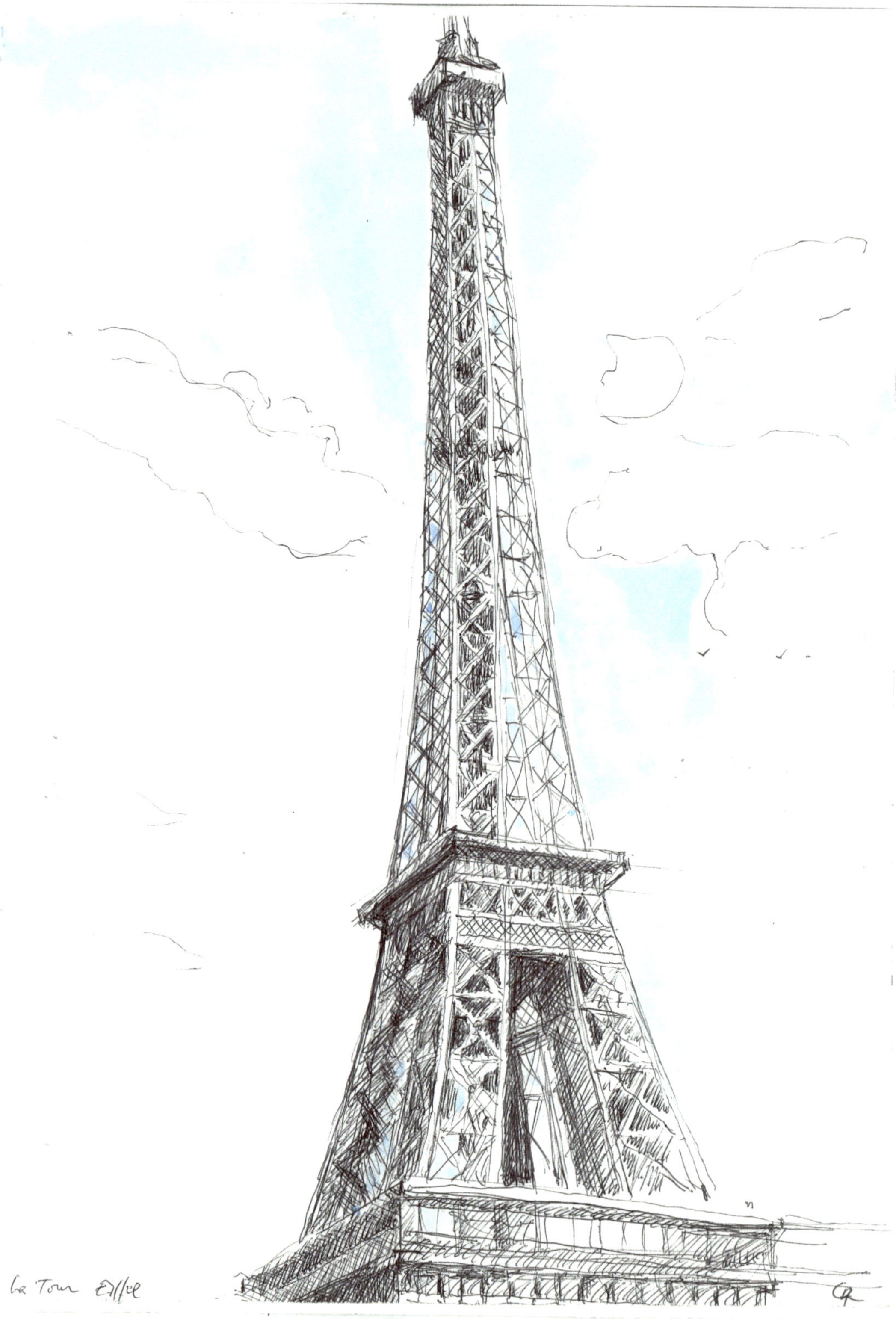

La Tour Eiffel

The Left Bank

ERNEST HEMINGWAY

If you are lucky enough to have lived in Paris as a young man, then wherever you go for the rest of your life, it stays with you, for Paris is a moveable feast.

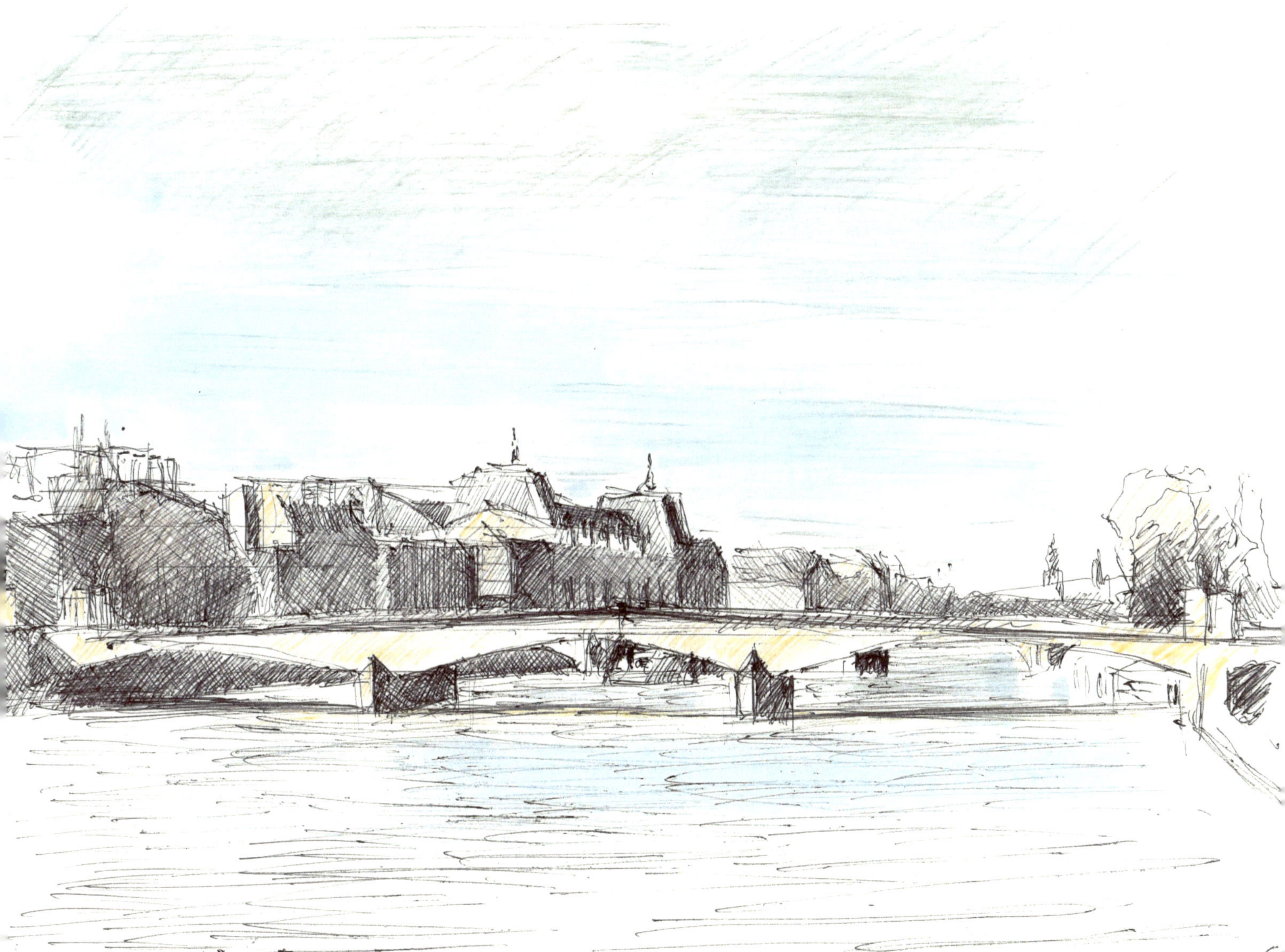

pont du Louvre – Musée d'Orsay

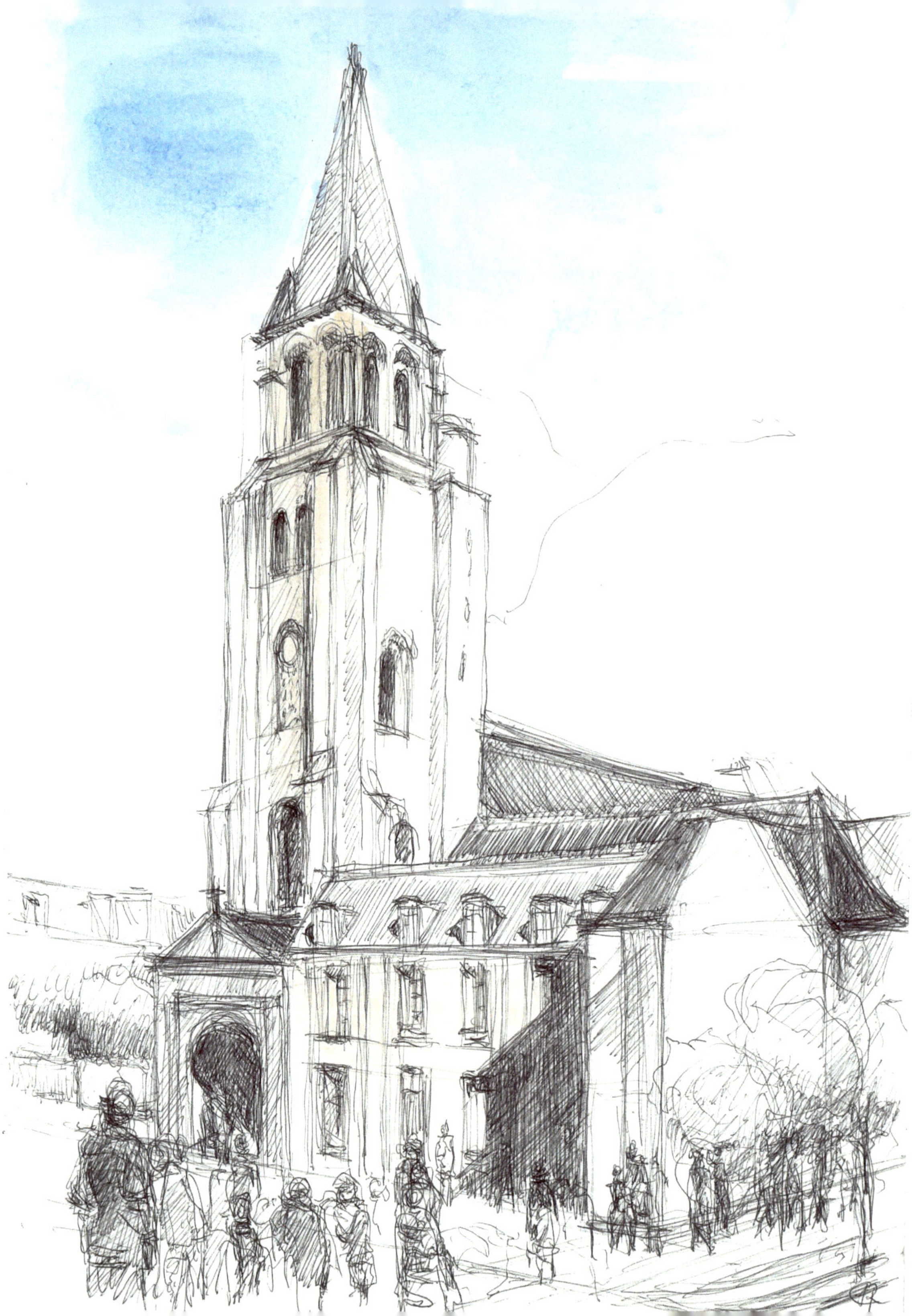

EDMUND WHITE

In Saint-Germain juries met to hand out literary prizes, movie deals were put together – and Sartre was introduced to Jean Genet for the first time on the terrace of Les Deux Magots. Le Corbusier, Giacometti, Picasso and the American Surrealist photographer Man Ray all hung out in Saint-Germain, partly because it was also near many of the galleries. Nightclubs such as La Rose Rouge and Le Tabou introduced bebop and *le jazz hot*.

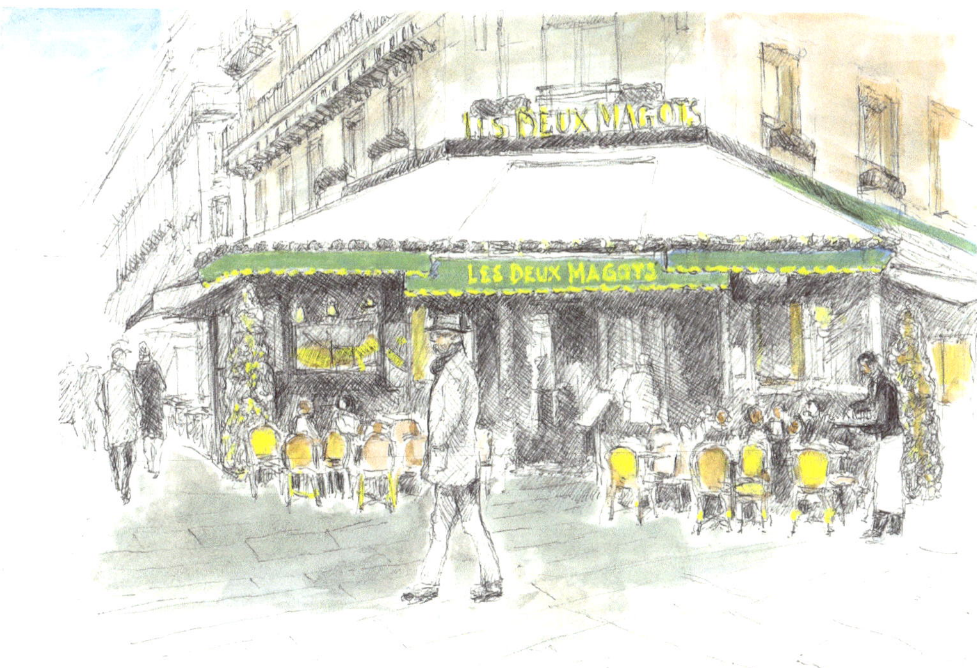

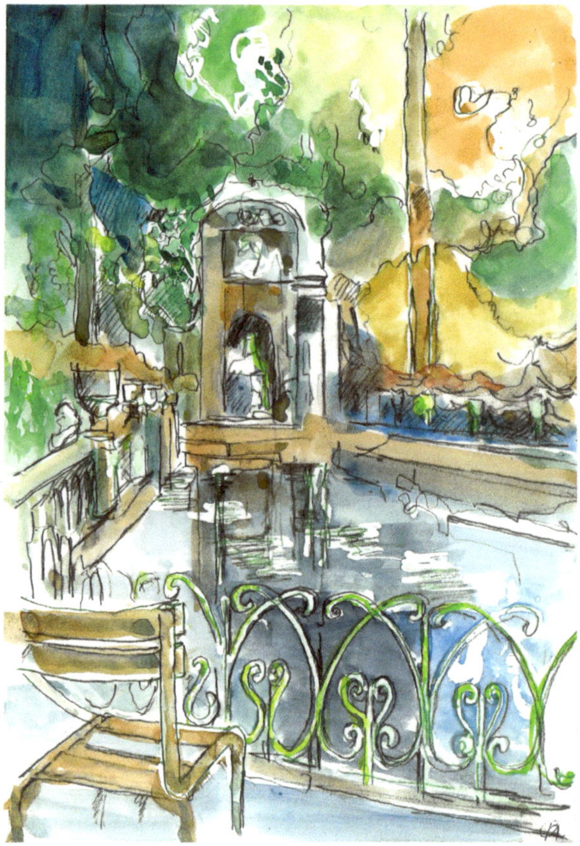

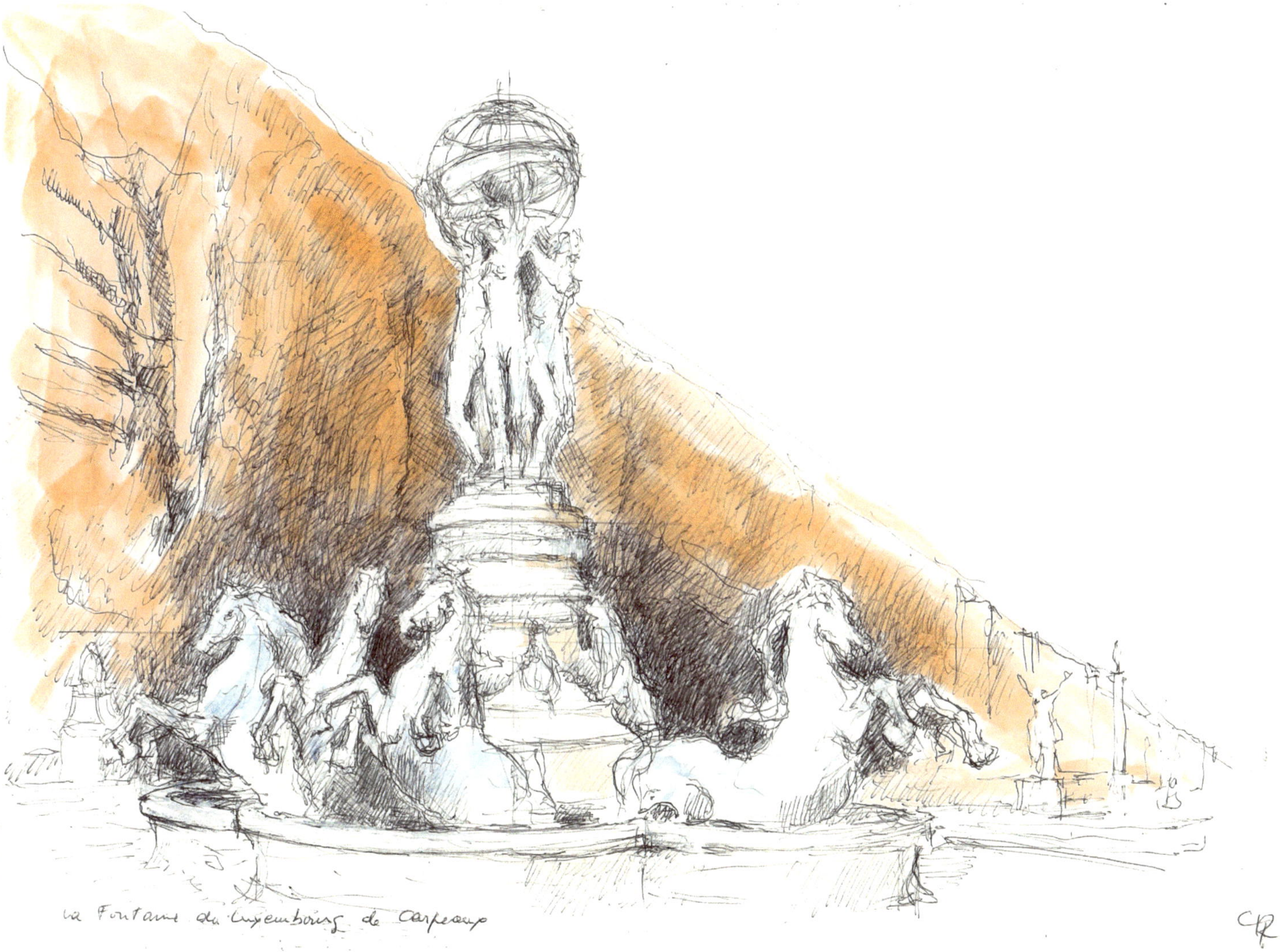
la Fontaine du Luxembourg de Carpeaux
CR

JULIEN GREEN

Just past there, Delacroix's studio in the tiny Furstemberg Square. The delightful sunken garden that is so good to sit in, shaded by trees on this fine summer's day, only yards from the deafening boulevard Saint-Germain. All around us, old houses with open windows, and those windows quite black. Watercolours by Delacroix, Huet, Reisener, Hugo, dreams in every direction. The oasis in our century that is so wretchedly devoid of poetry. A pale-blue sky above our heads, with clouds floating in it like puffs of steam.

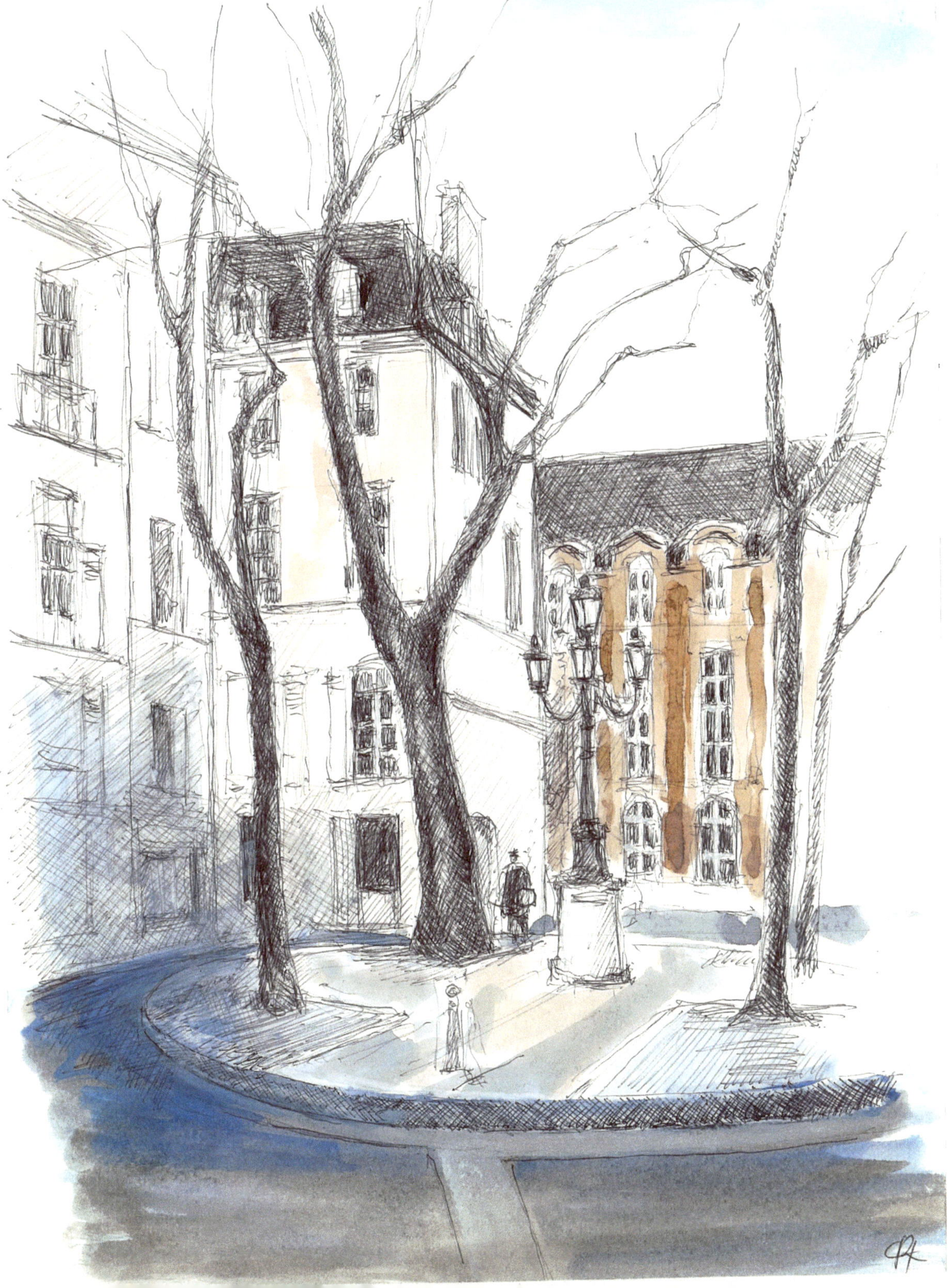

JULIEN GREEN

Everything in this city has a quality that defies analysis but enables you to say without hesitation: 'That is Paris' – even if it is only a milk can dangling from a door knob, or one of those coarse brooms sweeping up the leaves at the pavement's edge in October with a sound like the sea, or an array of tired-looking volumes in a bookseller's box on the embankment between the Pont Neuf and the Pont Royal. Why this should be so I do not know, but Paris sets its seal on everything that belongs to it.

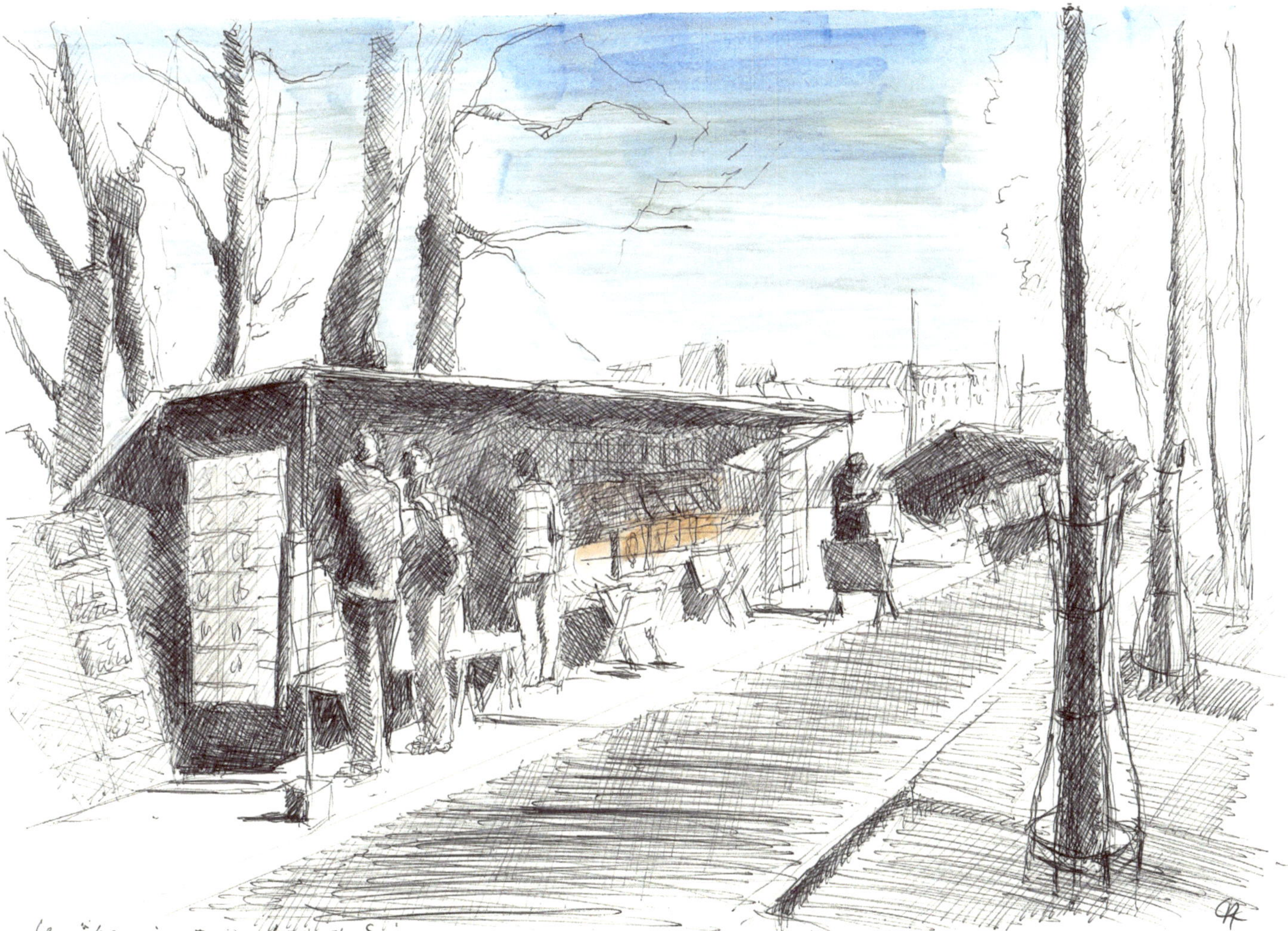

Les "bouquinistes" bord de Seine.

LOUIS ARAGON

Nothing has the sparkle of Paris ignited
Nothing's so pure as her rebel raised head
Nothing so strong - not fire, not thunder -
As Paris thumbing her nose at danger
Nothing so beautiful as this Paris of mine.

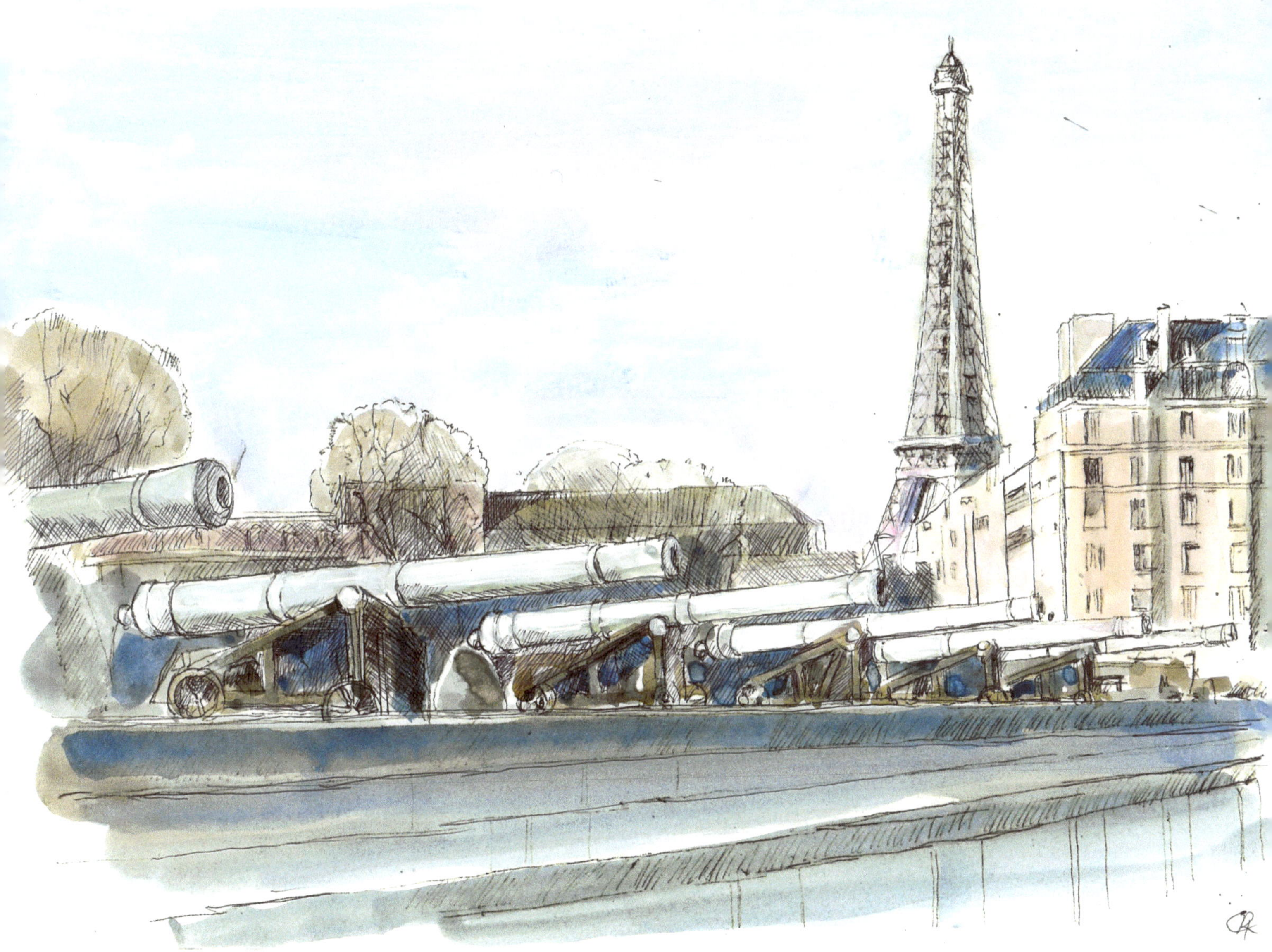

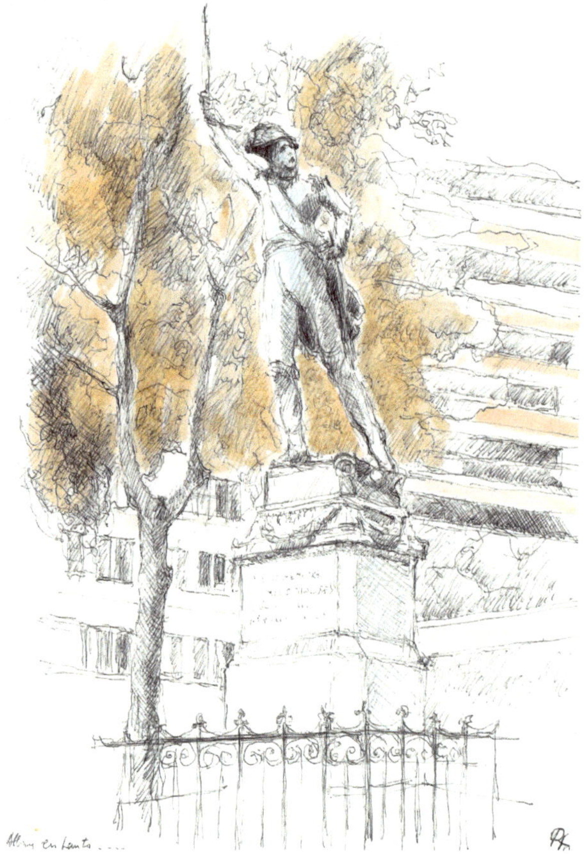
Allons enfants . . . .

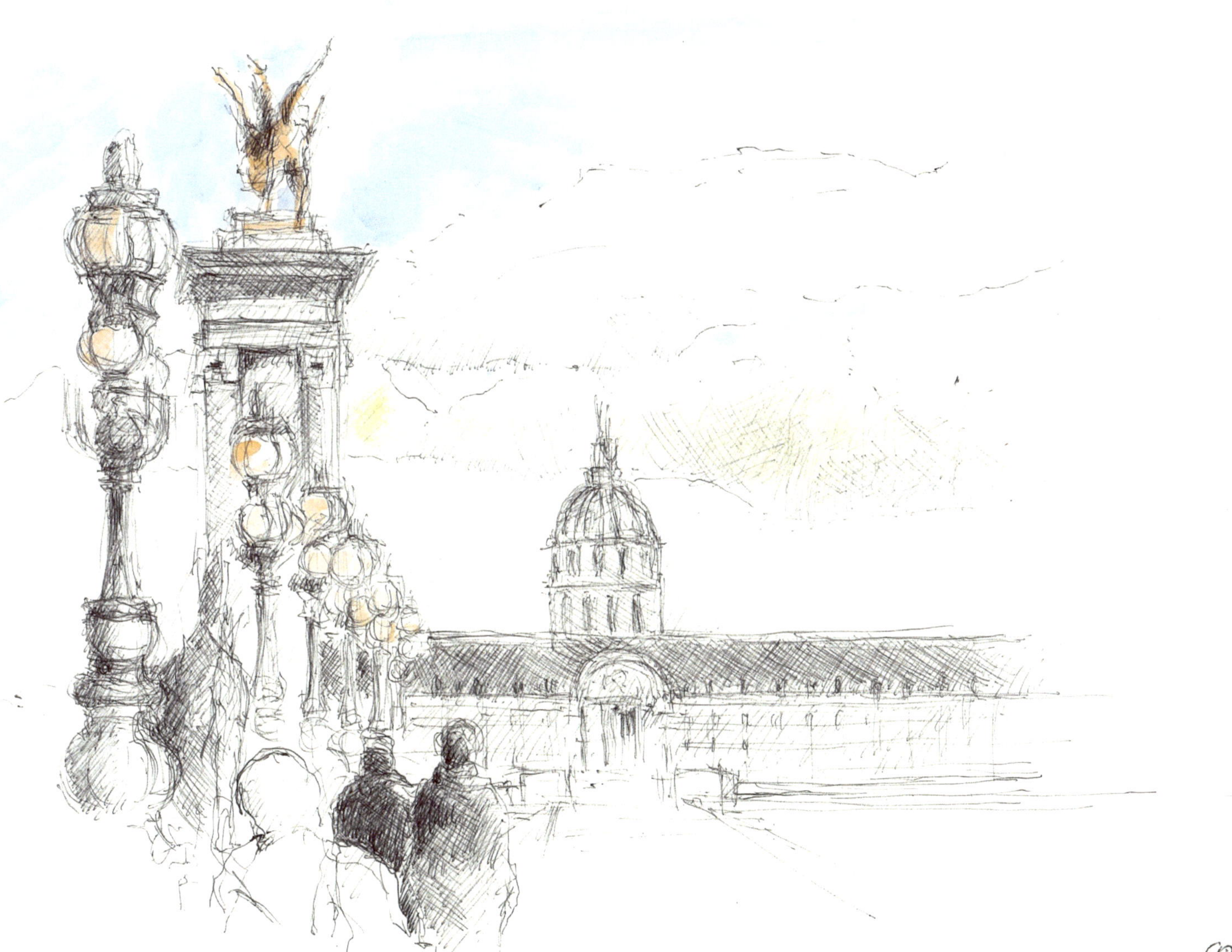

Les Invalides depuis le pont Alexandre III

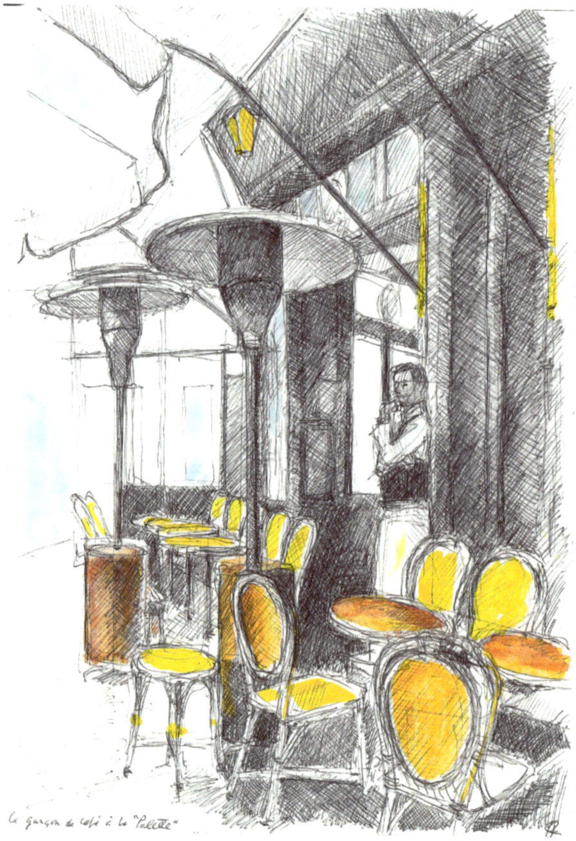
Le garçon de café à la "Palette"

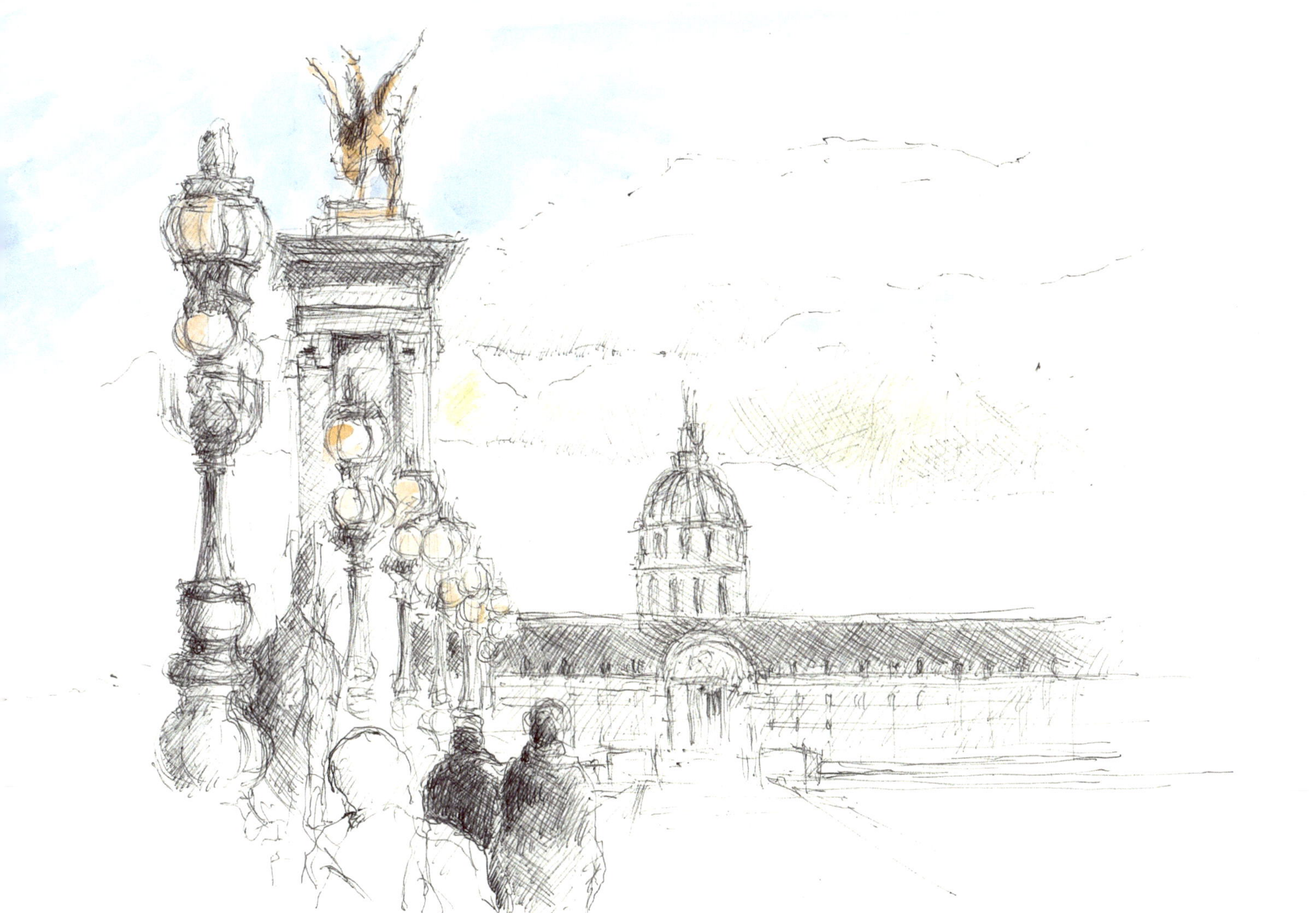

Les Invalides depuis le pont Alexandre III

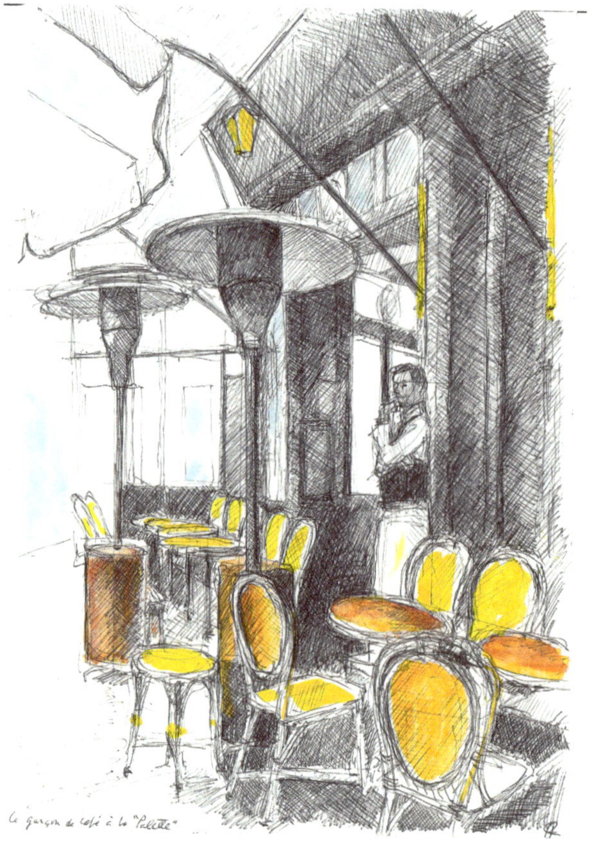
Le garçon de café à la "Palette"

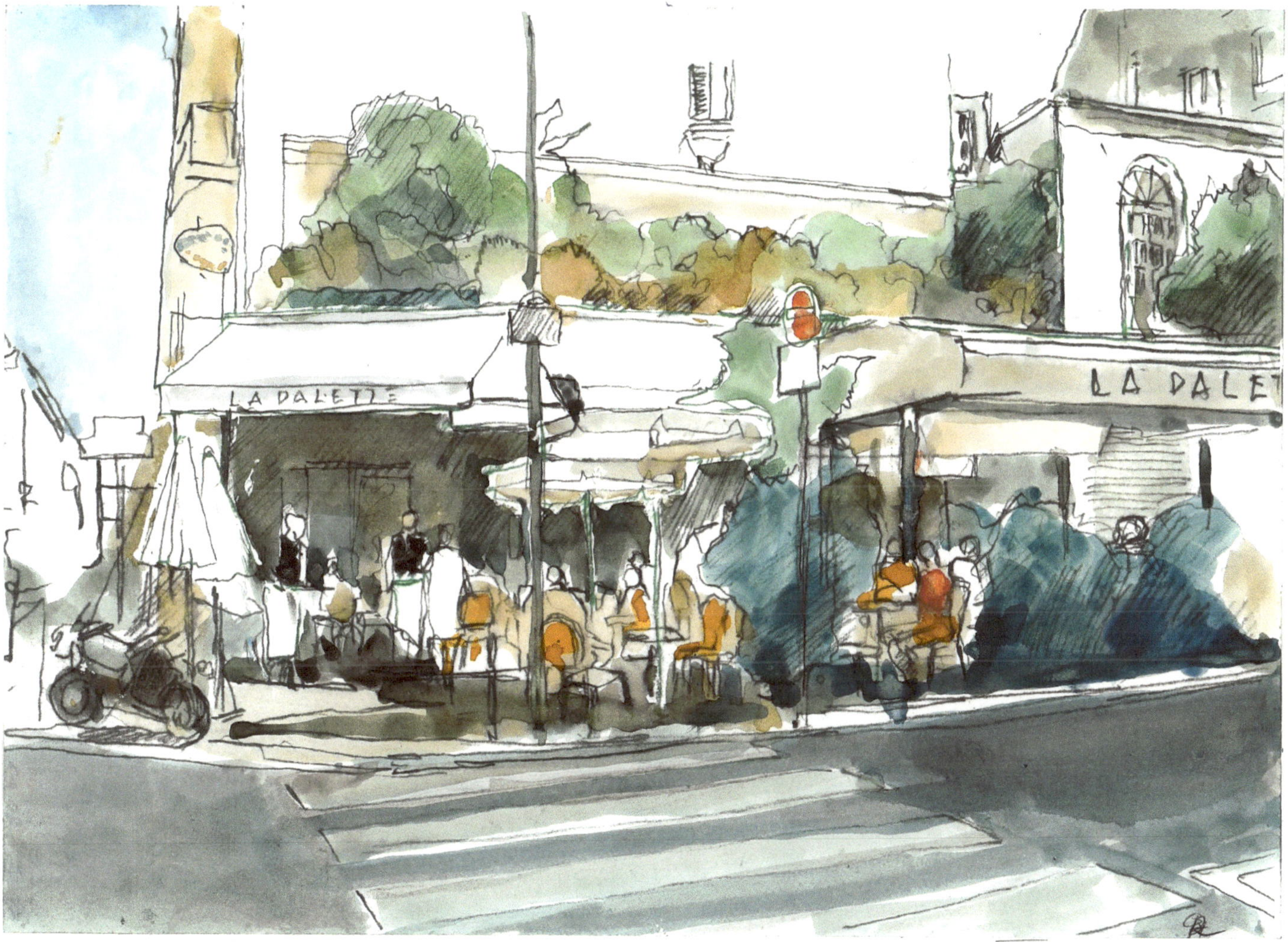

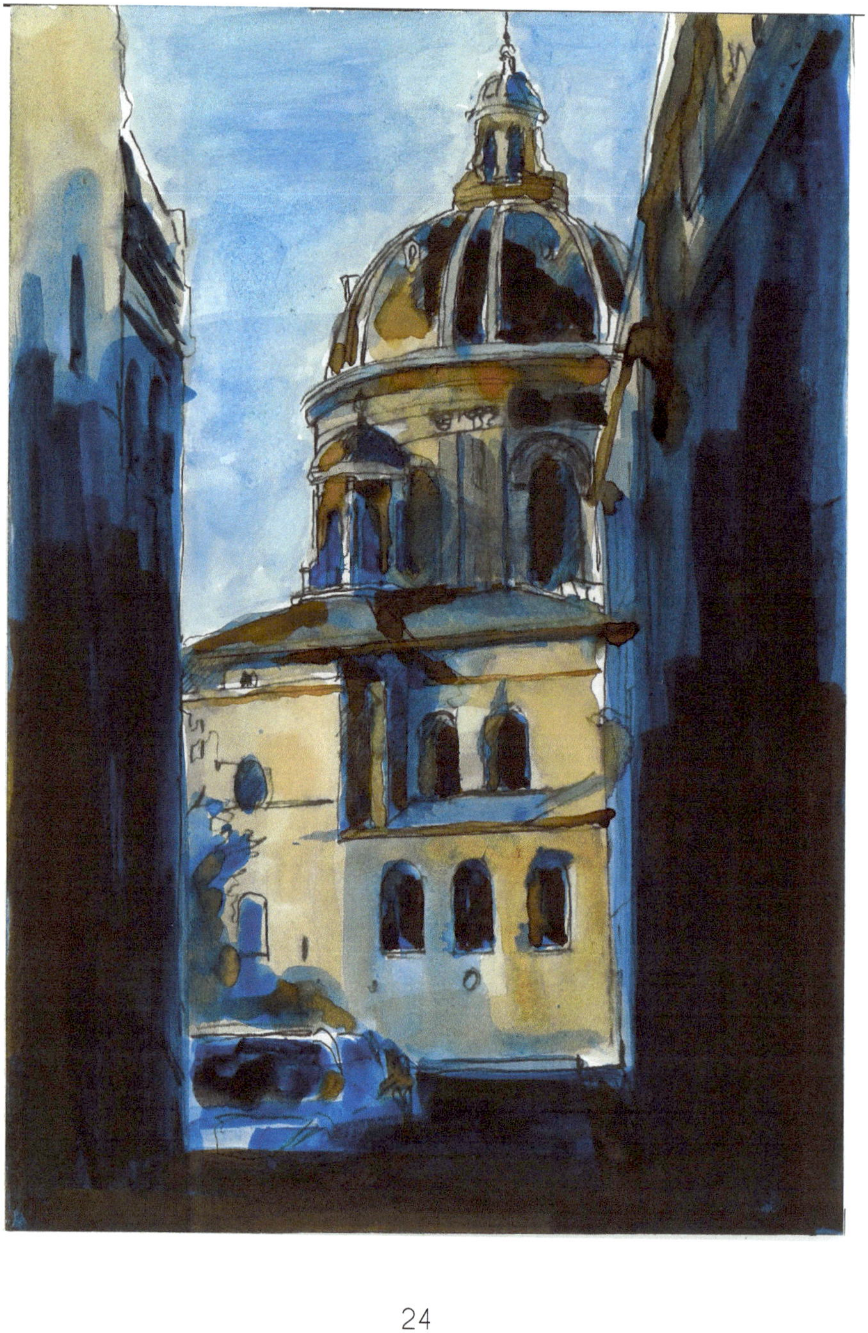

ANDRÉ FRÉNAUD

O Paris, my bitter
blue almond
my pensive reserve,
down to the stones
of your breast
my sweet grasses
you hawkers of colour
trees of my uttering voice
and your spoiling sky
o my enchanted helmet.

JULIEN GREEN

Paris is a city that might well be spoken of in the plural, as the Greeks used to speak of Athens, for there are many Parises, and the tourists' Paris is only superficially related to the Paris of the Parisians. The foreigner driving through the city from one museum to another is quite oblivious to the presence of a world he brushes past without seeing. Until you have wasted time in a city, you cannot pretend to know it well. The soul of the big city is not to be grasped so easily; in order to make contact with it, you have to have been bored, you have to have suffered a bit in those places that contain it. Anyone can get hold of a guide and tick off all the monuments, but within the very confines of Paris there is another city as difficult of access as Timbuktu once was.

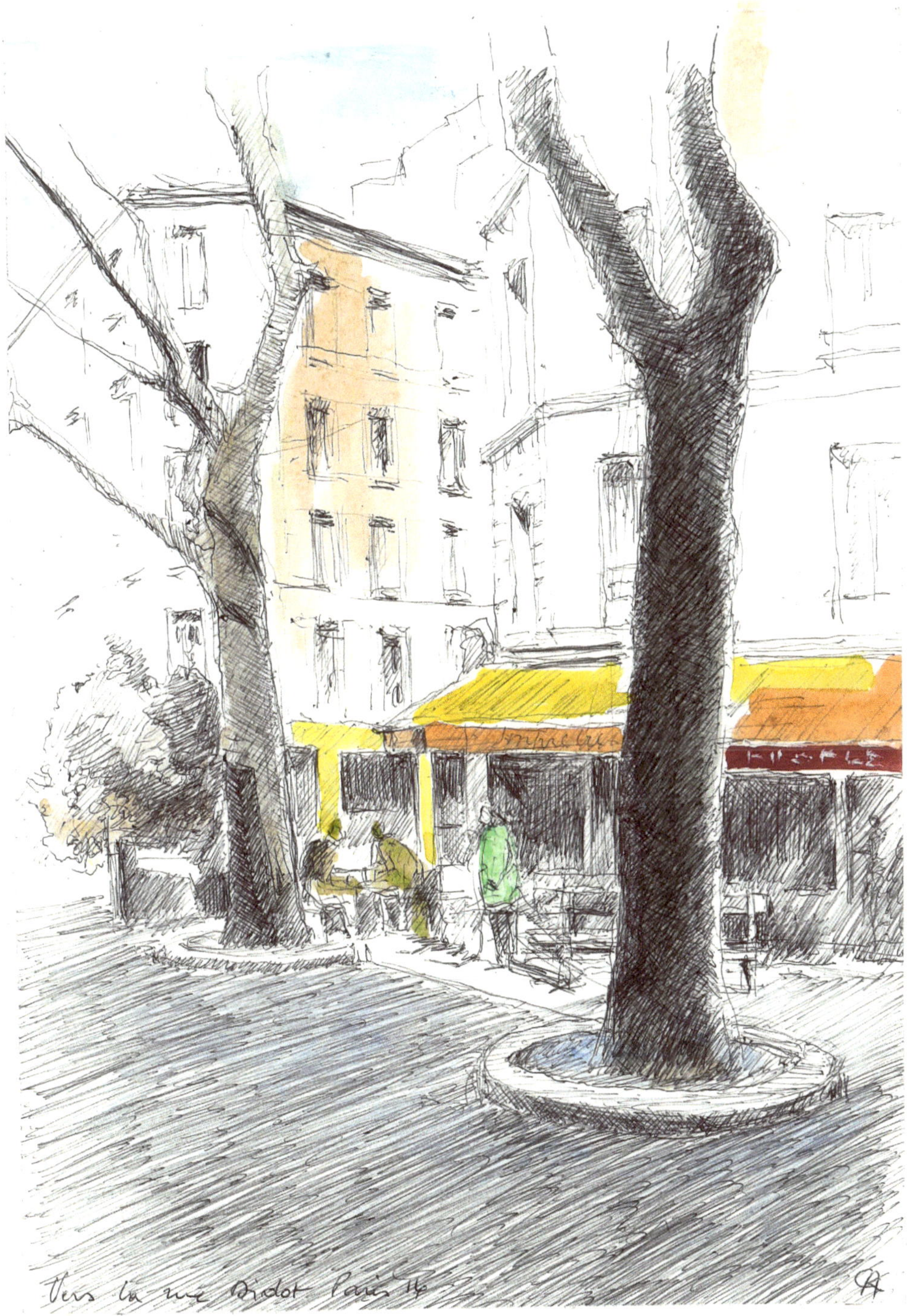
Vers la rue Didot Paris 14

JAMES JOYCE

Paris rawly waking, crude sunlight on her lemon streets. Moist pith of farls of bread, the froggreen wormwood, her matin incense, court the air… Faces of Paris men go by, their wellpleased pleasers, curled conquistadores.

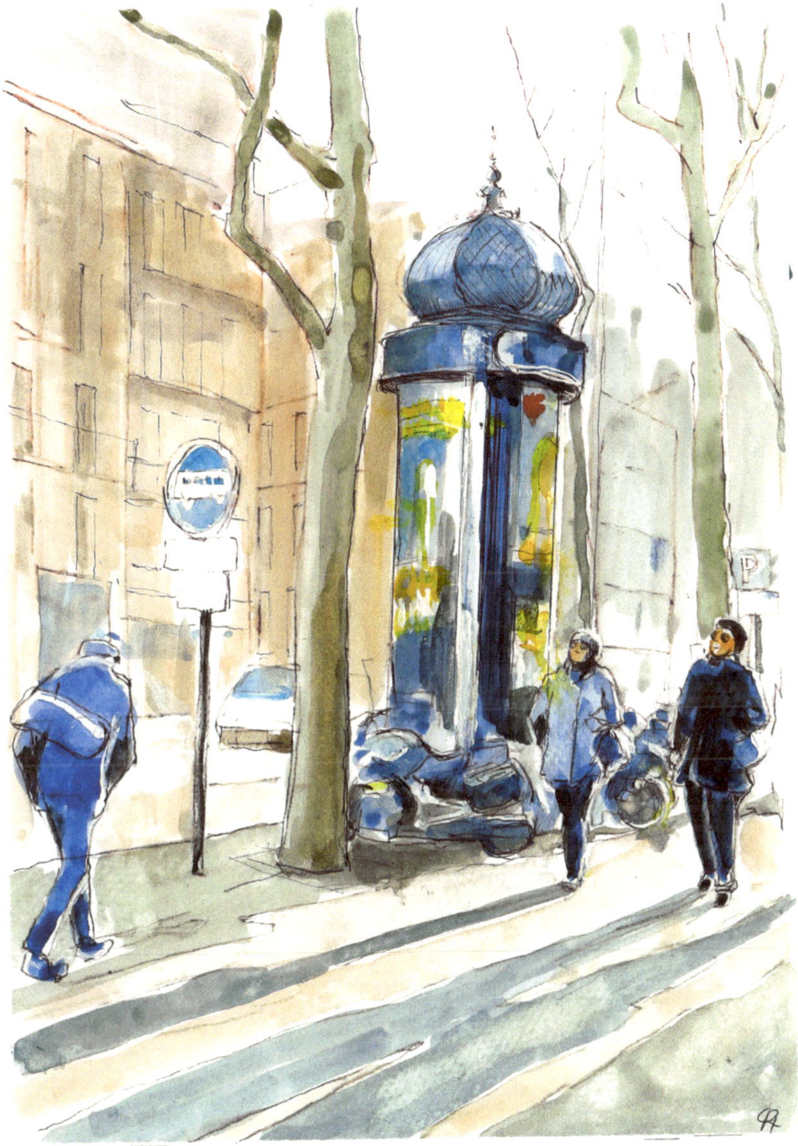

ELISABETH BARRET BROWING

And trade is art, and art's philosophy,
In Paris.

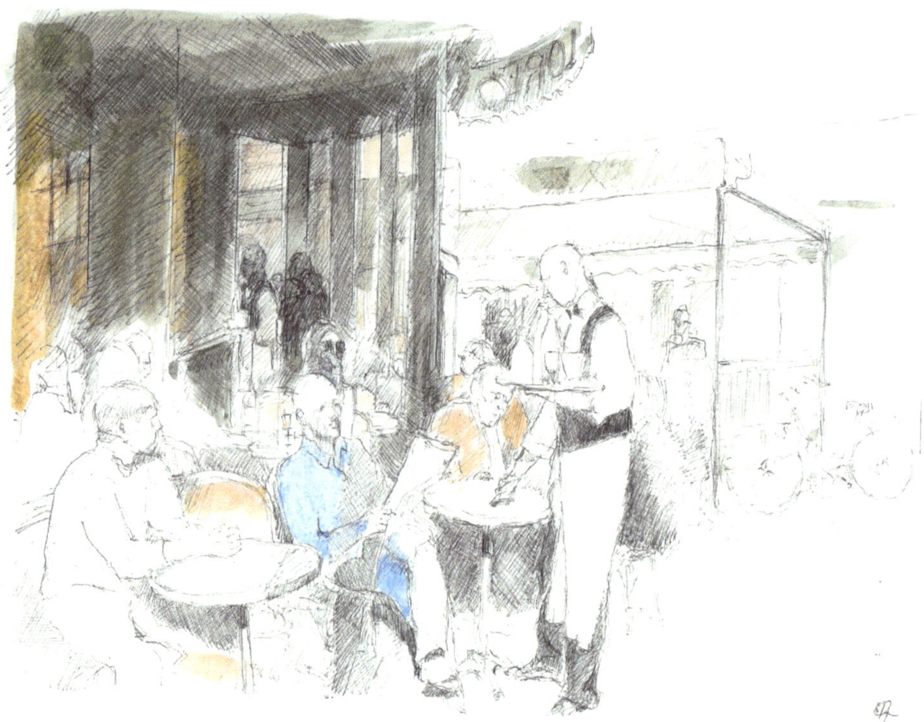

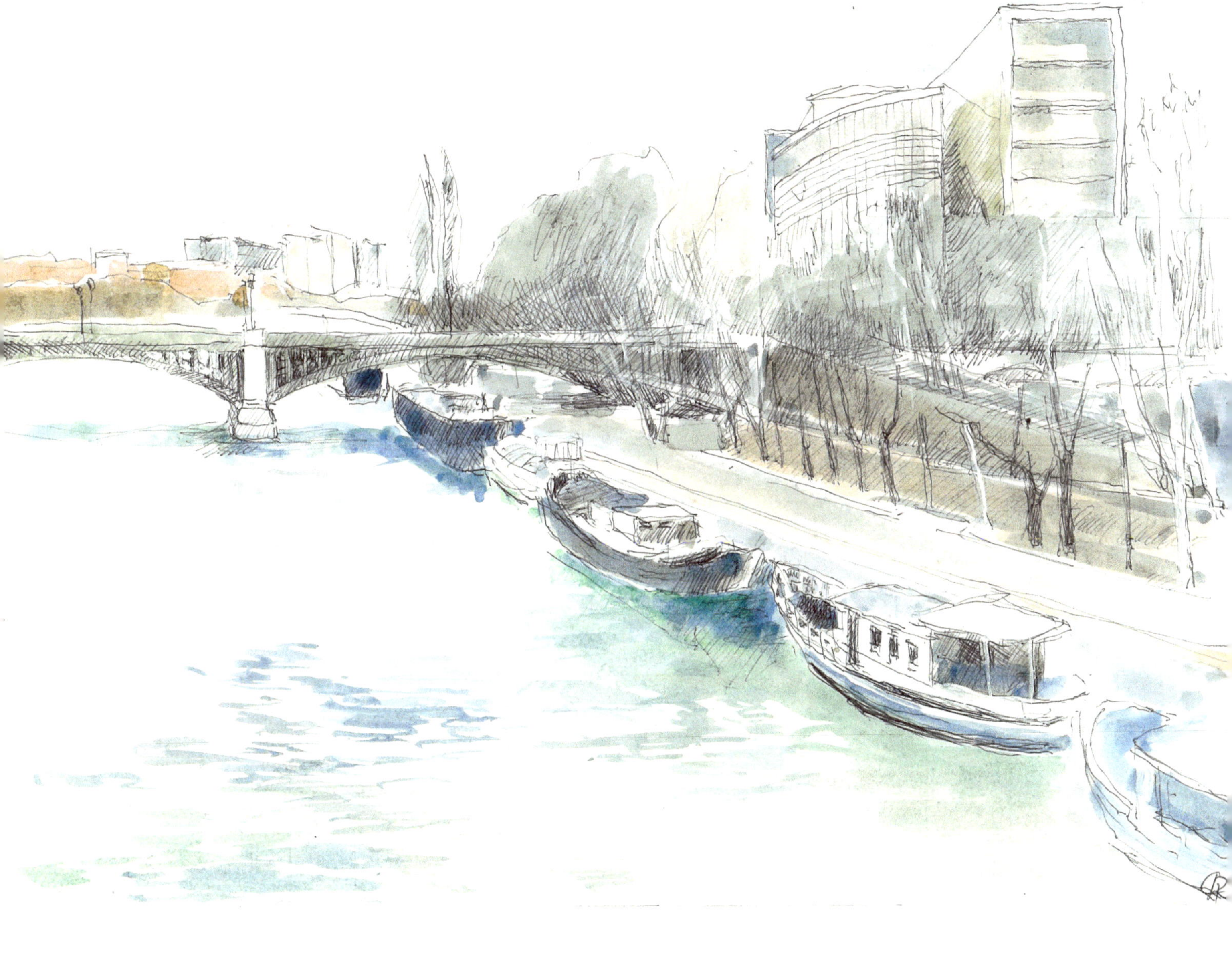

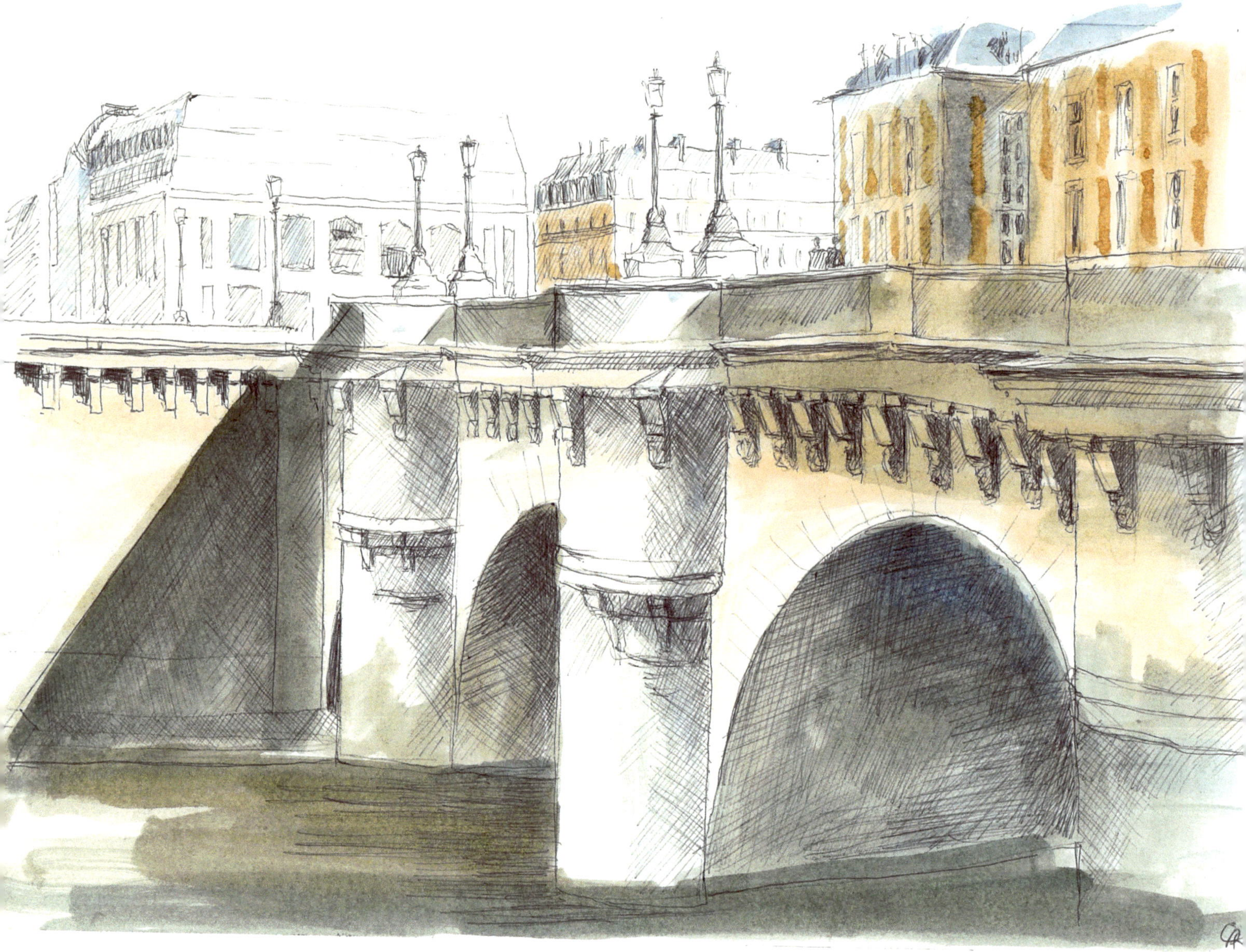

The River Seine and the islands Cité and Saint-Louis

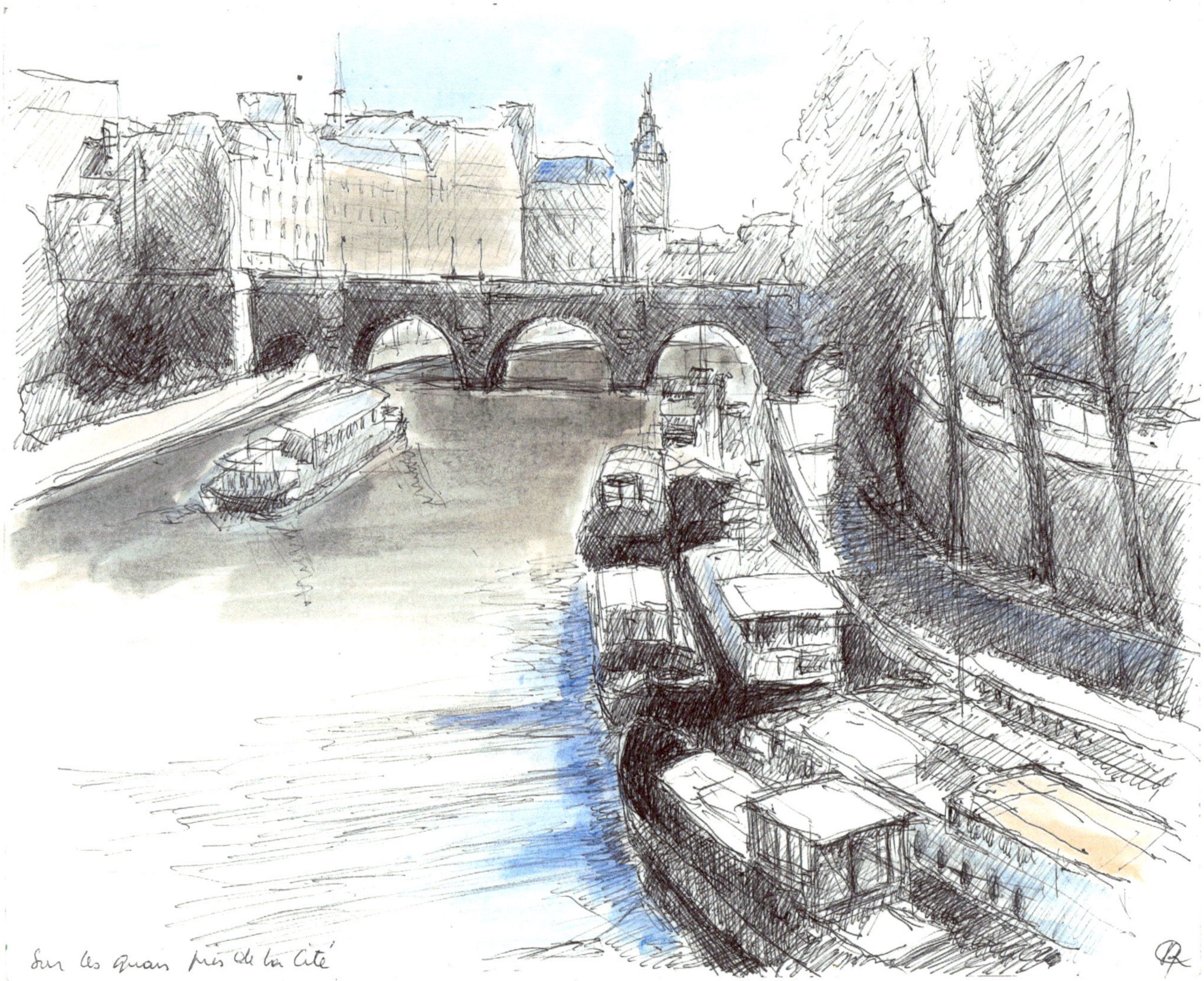
Sur les quais près de la Cité

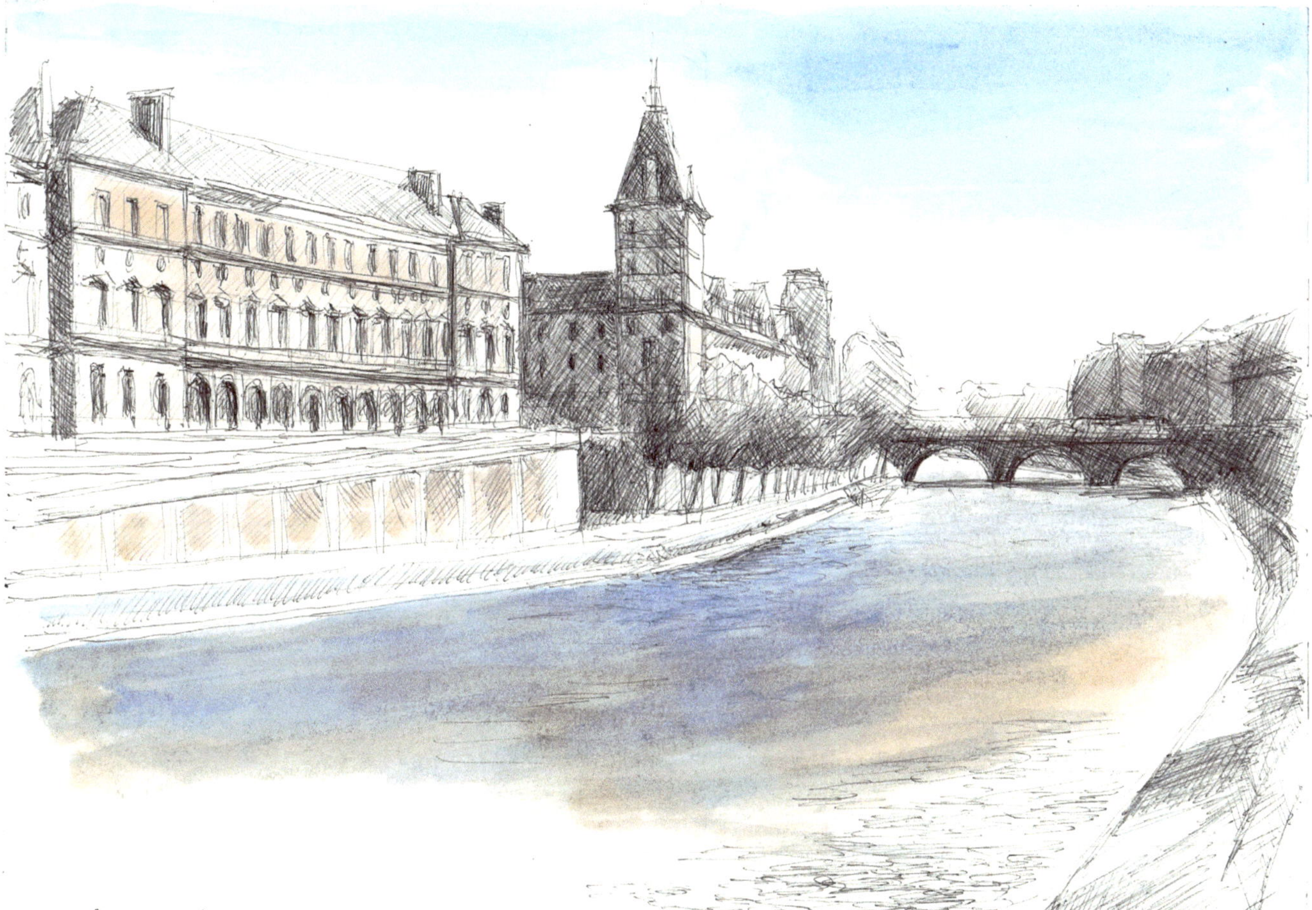

Quai des orfèvres - Ile de la Cité. La conciergerie

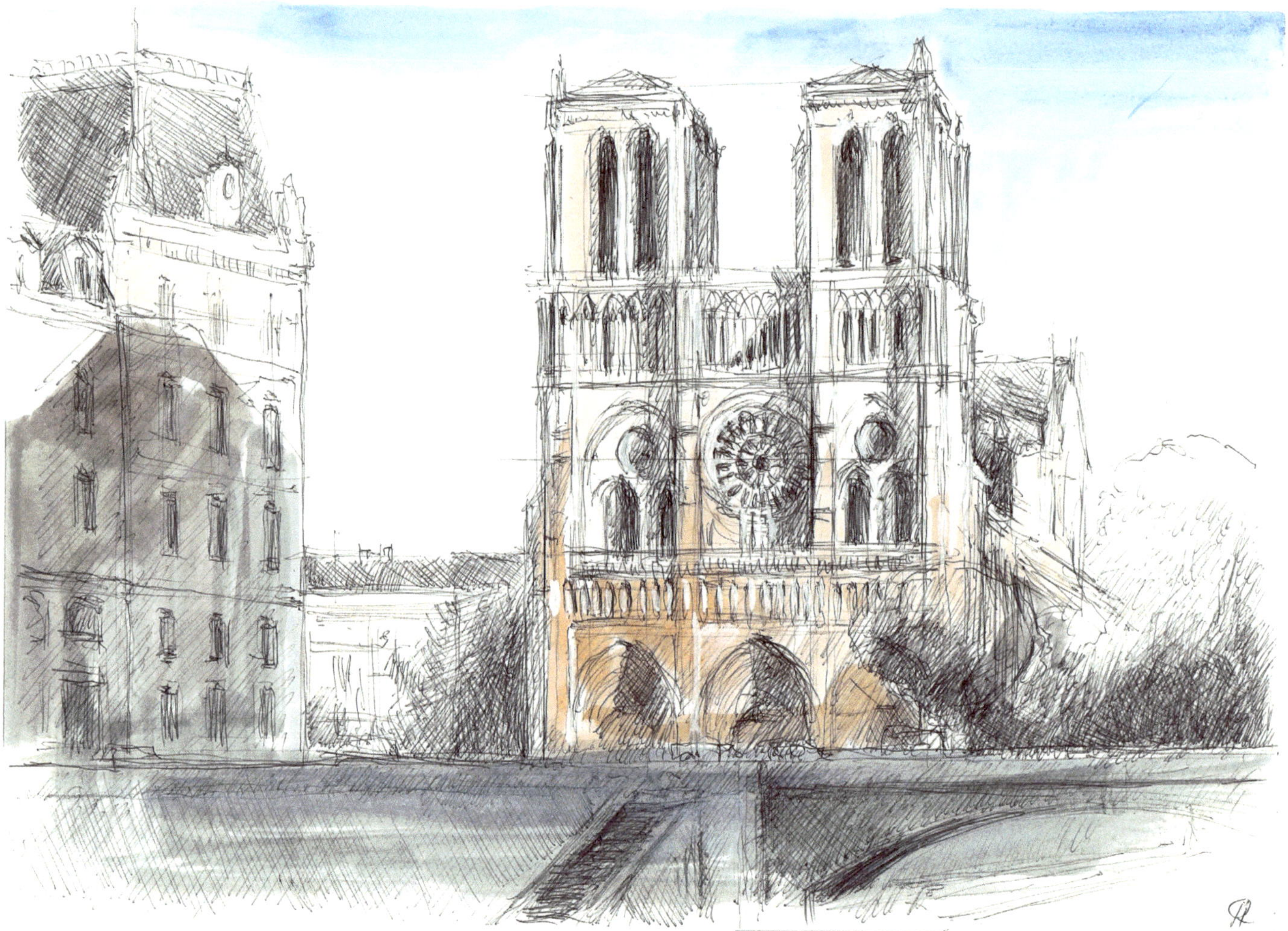

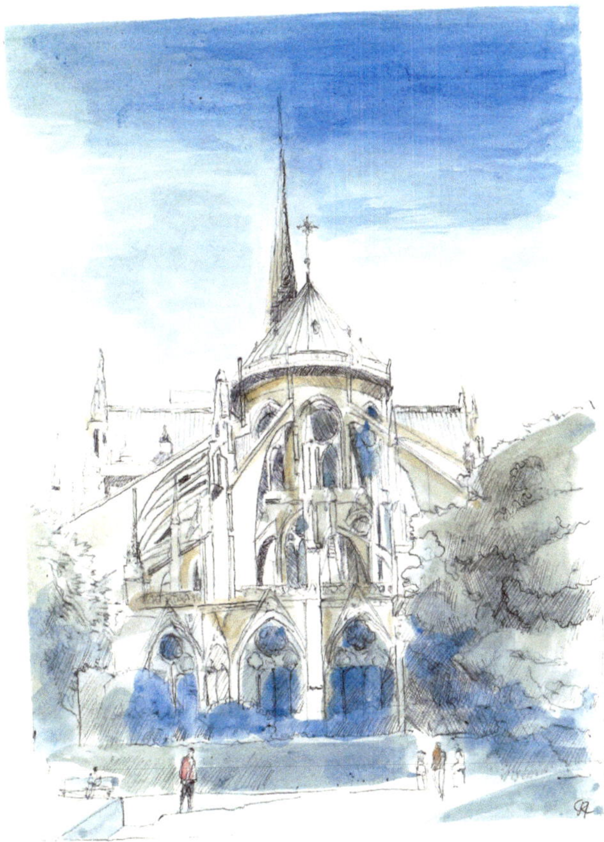

JANELLE MCCULLOCH

The rain, which had fallen lightly like pearl-gray tulle through the night, had stopped, although the streetlamps still shone like Cartier diamonds in the pale light. And everywhere you looked, there was a compelling beauty that made the 'oh' catch in your throat. The city was, in all its autumnal splendour, a romantic pastiche of poetic gestures, and it was perfect. Just perfect. The kind of day that makes you believe the ideal can be real.

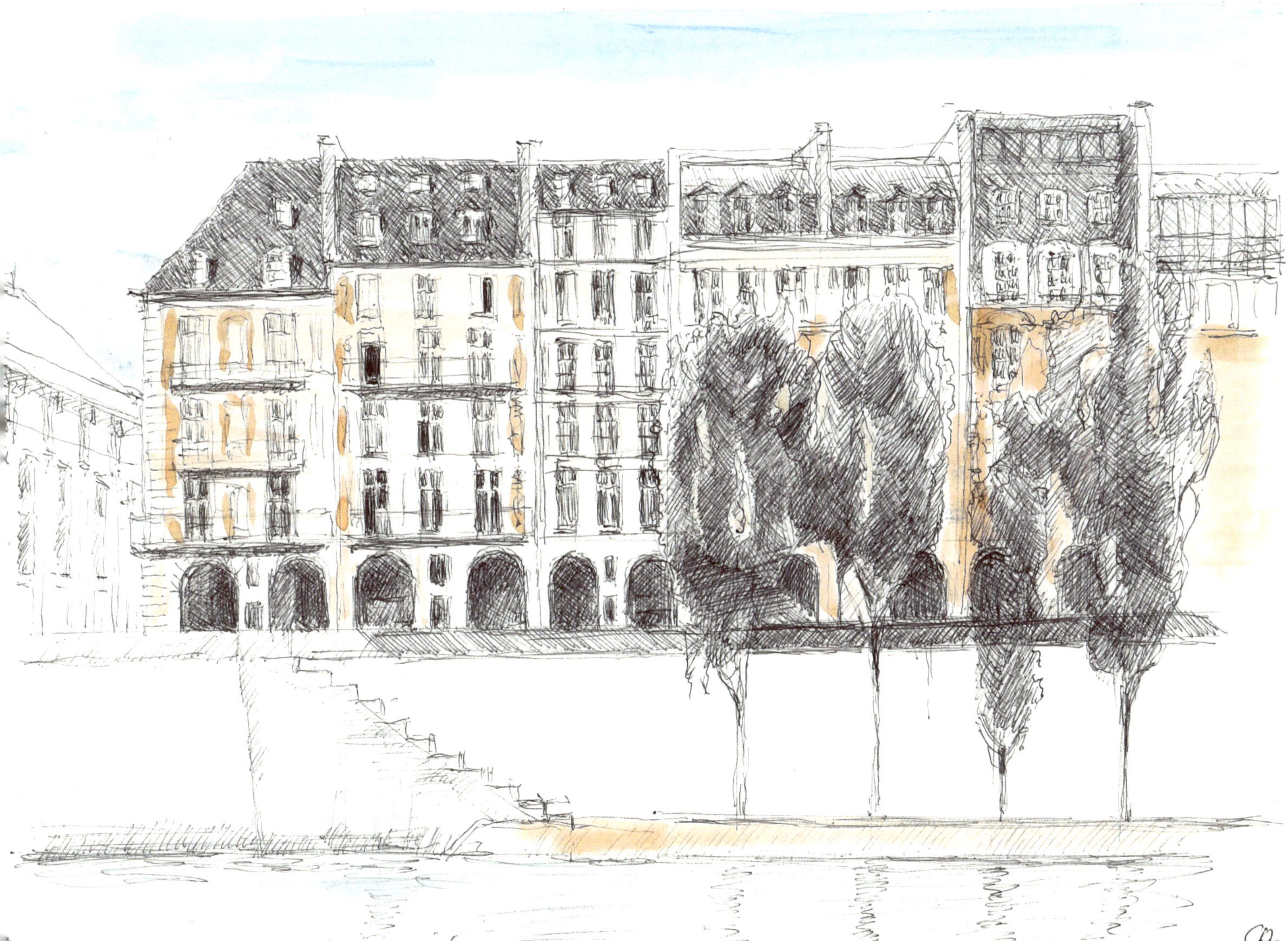

mmeubles "parisiens" dans l'Ile de la Cité

JACQUES BREL

Paris in love
As we raise our first glass
On the Île Saint-Louis
Paris a wish
As we steal a first kiss
On a bridge in the sun
Paris begun

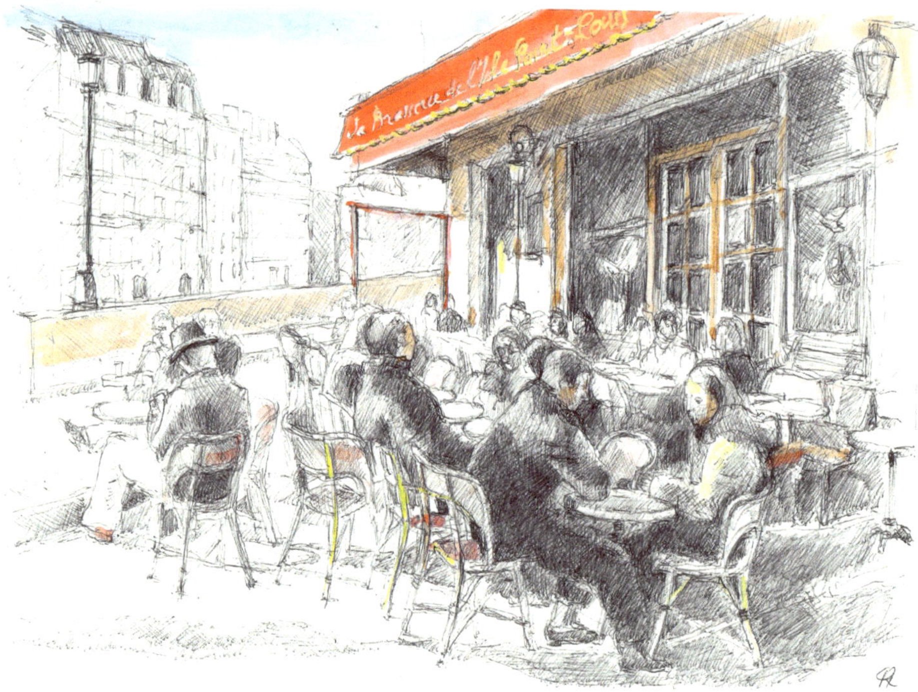

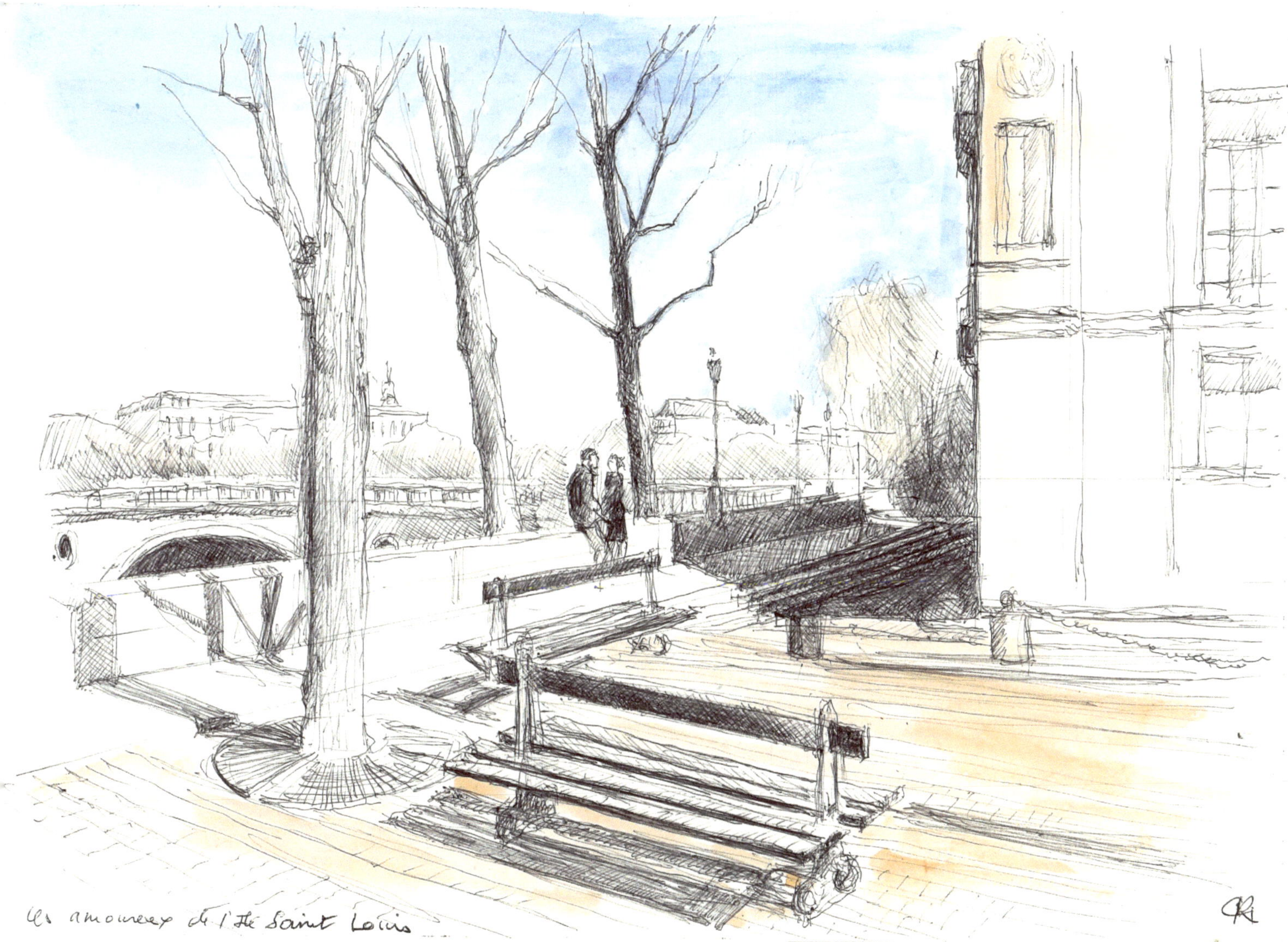
Les amoureux de l'Ile Saint Louis

SARAH TURNBULL

The colours and light are Monetesque – smudged golden-pink skies and soft violet shadows. Now I see why artists and writers have compared Paris light to champagne. The evening air does have an effervescent quality. On the quai below, couples fall into each other's arms. I don't think I've ever seen such a meltingly romantic setting.

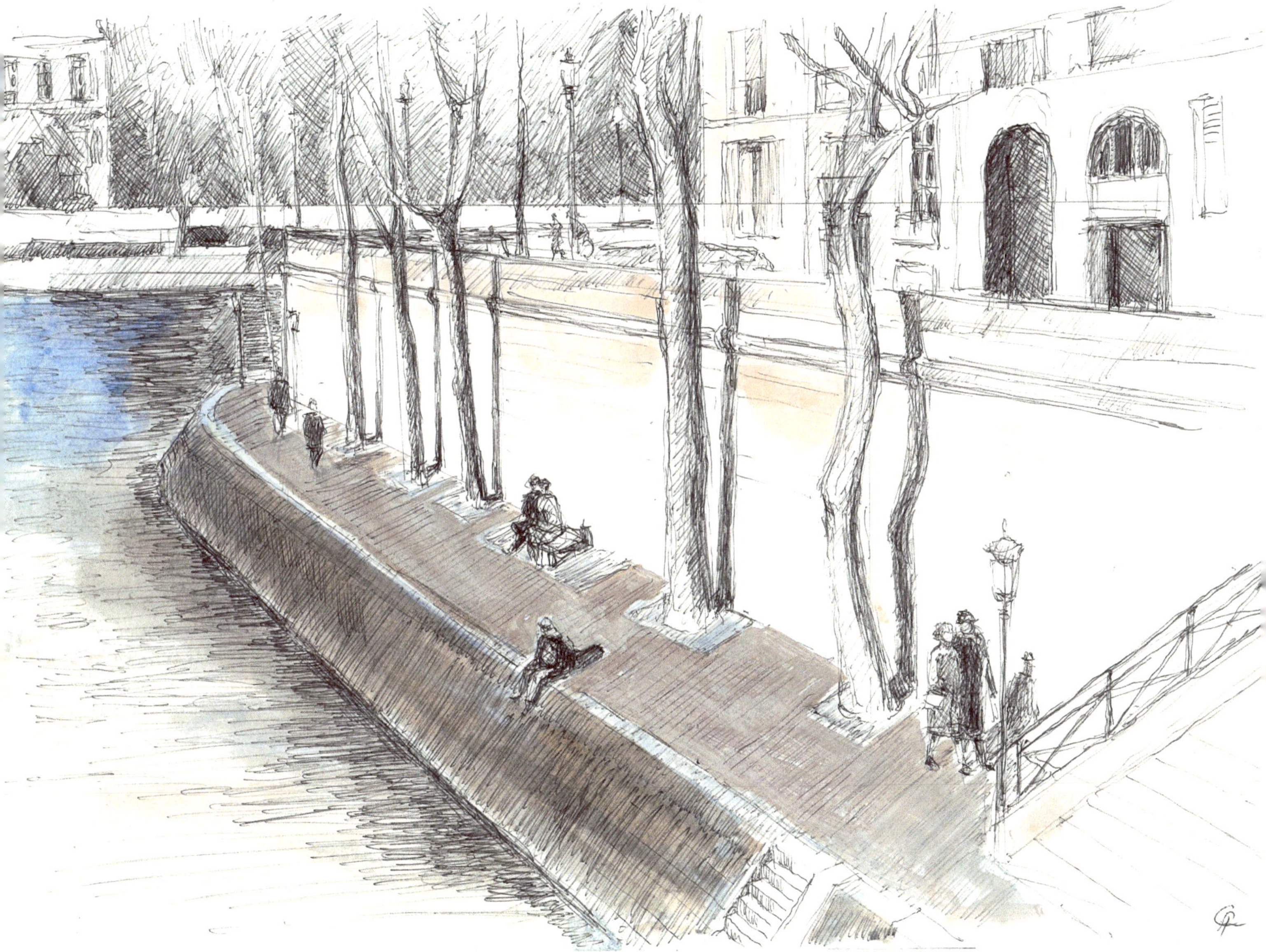

JANELLE MCCULLOCH

Most people don't realise that Paris is more beautiful going into the colder months than any other time. Under a dignified sky of Dior grey, you can see the 'bones' of the city, including its noble architecture, through the brittle branches of the trees. Somehow, the city seems finer, grander, more spectacular.

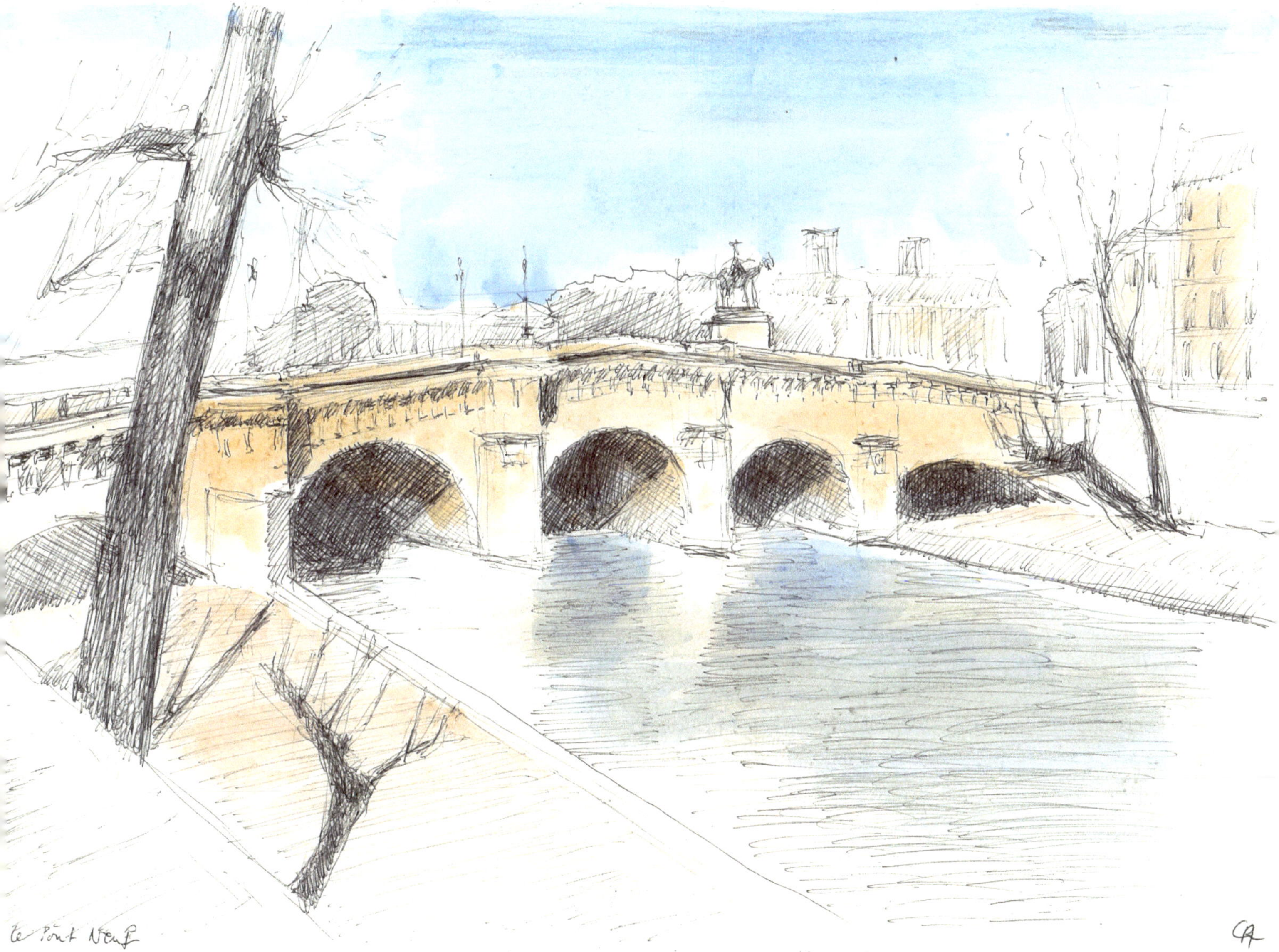
le Pont Neuf

BLAISE CENDRARS

This Paris sky, cleaner than winter sky lucid with cold...

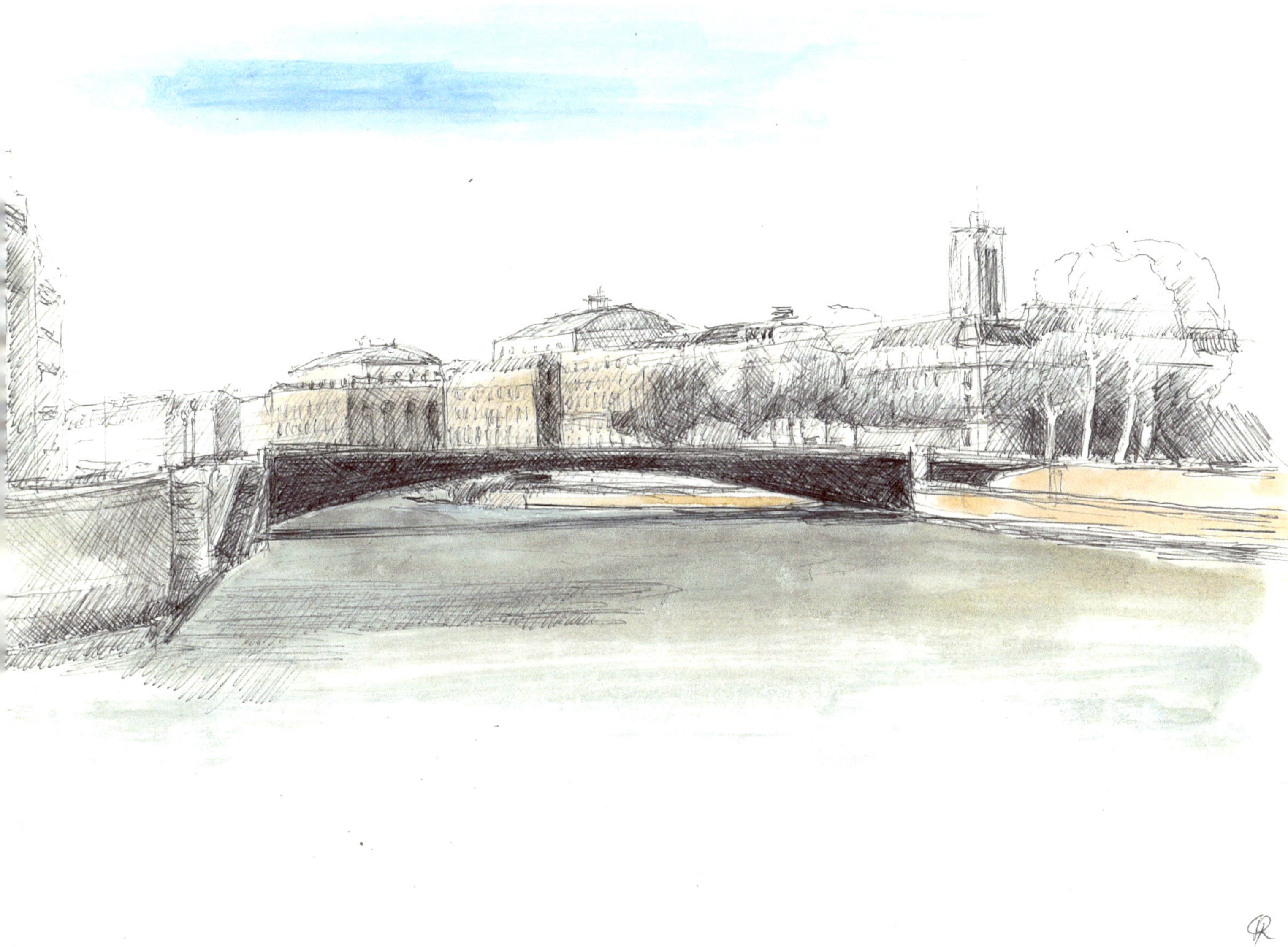

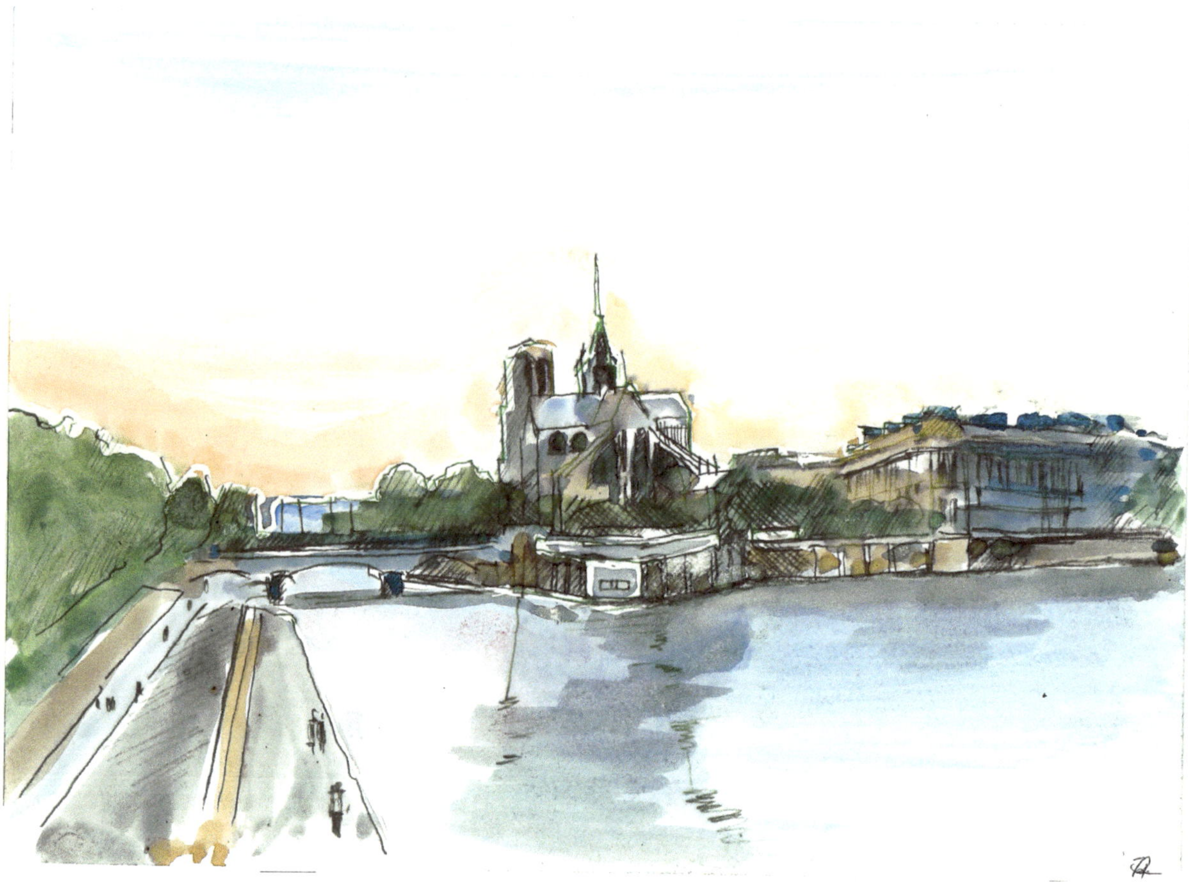

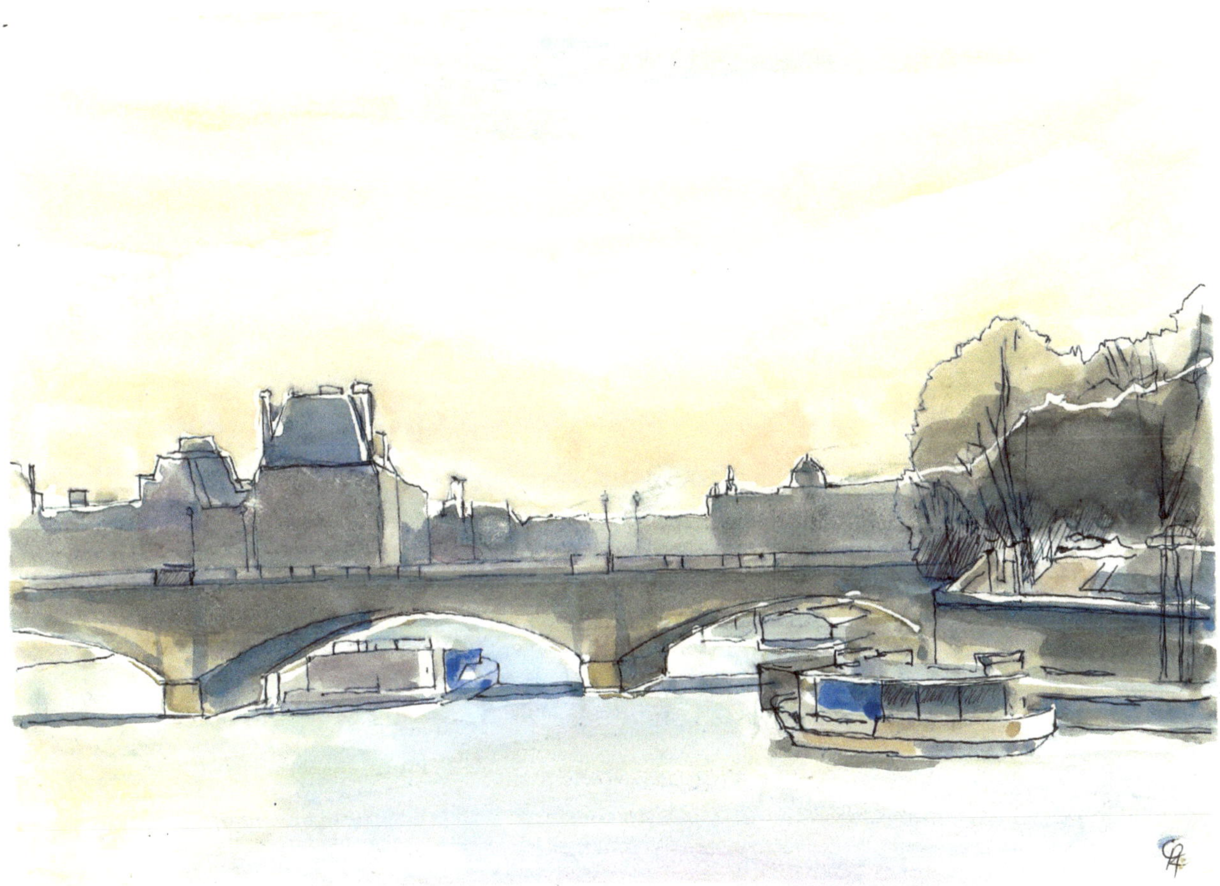

CRAIG McDONALD

I fell in love with Ernest Hemingway's vision of Paris as a very young man upon a first reading of *A Moveable Feast*. I long nursed this notion of running off to the City of Lights to live Hemingway's memoir. I finally made it to Paris in my forties. It'd been a long time since Hemingway, apprentice author, limped her streets. A hell of a lot of water had coursed under all those picturesque bridges joining her banks. Yet she remains immortal in her way, very much the city Hem loved. An old maxim has it Paris, like an ageless femme fatale, "Will kiss you or kill you, but she will never bore you". As Hemingway wrote of Paris long after he'd left her, 'She is like a mistress who does not grow old and she has other lovers now... she is always the same age and she always has new lovers'.

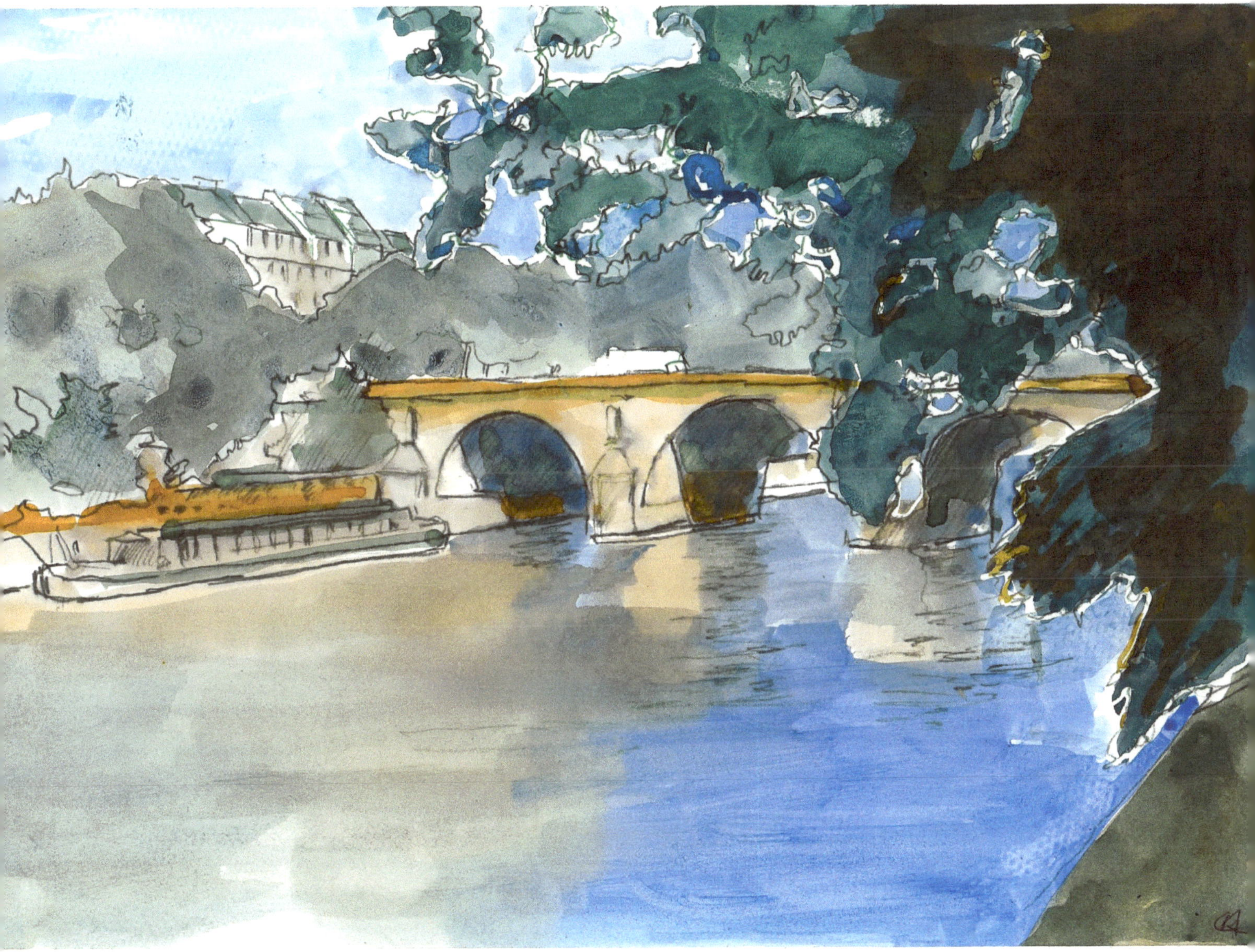

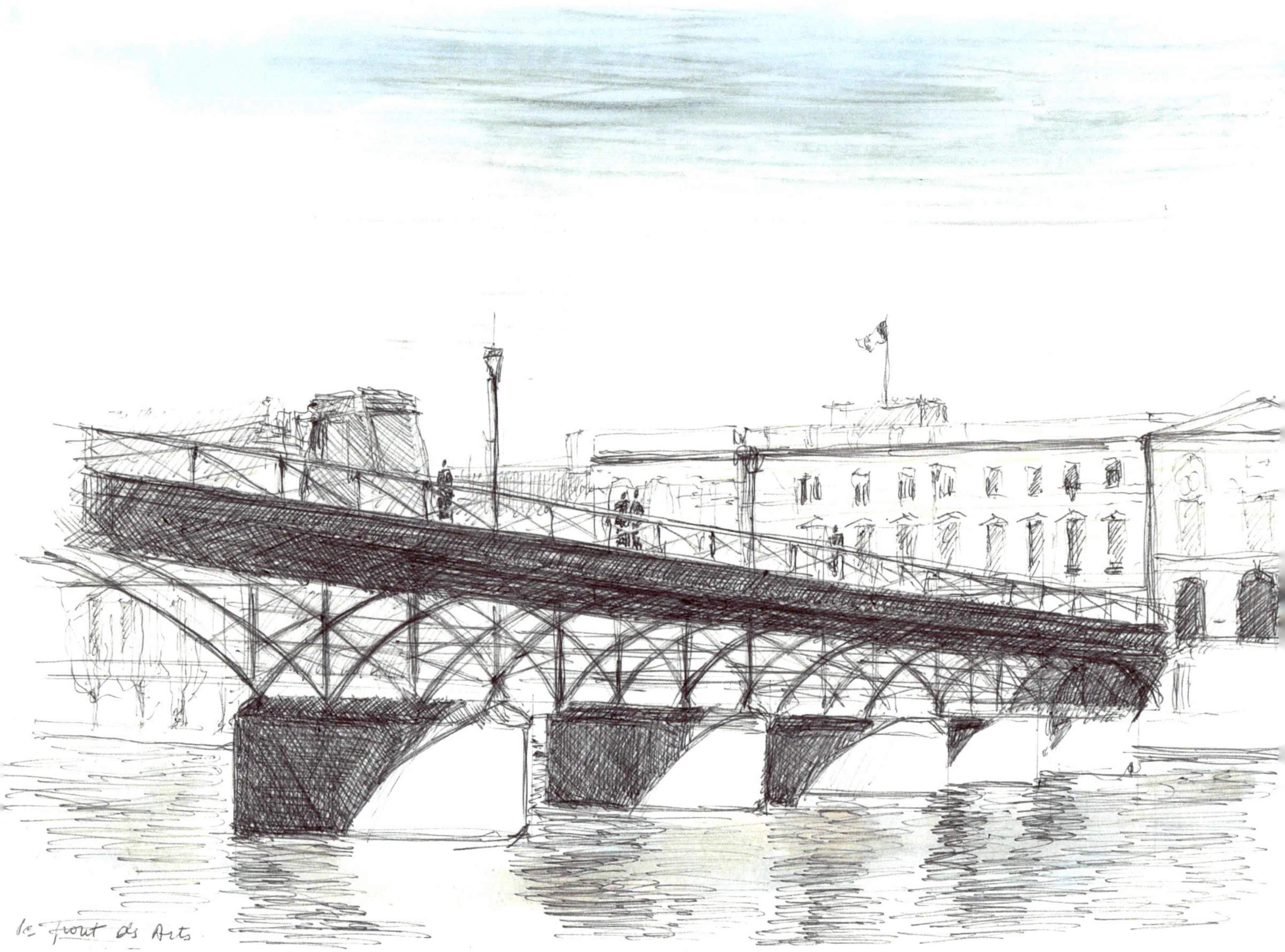
le pont des Arts

The Right Bank

VICTOR HUGO

He who contemplates the depths of Paris is seized with vertigo.
Nothing is more fantastic. Nothing is more tragic.
Nothing is more sublime.

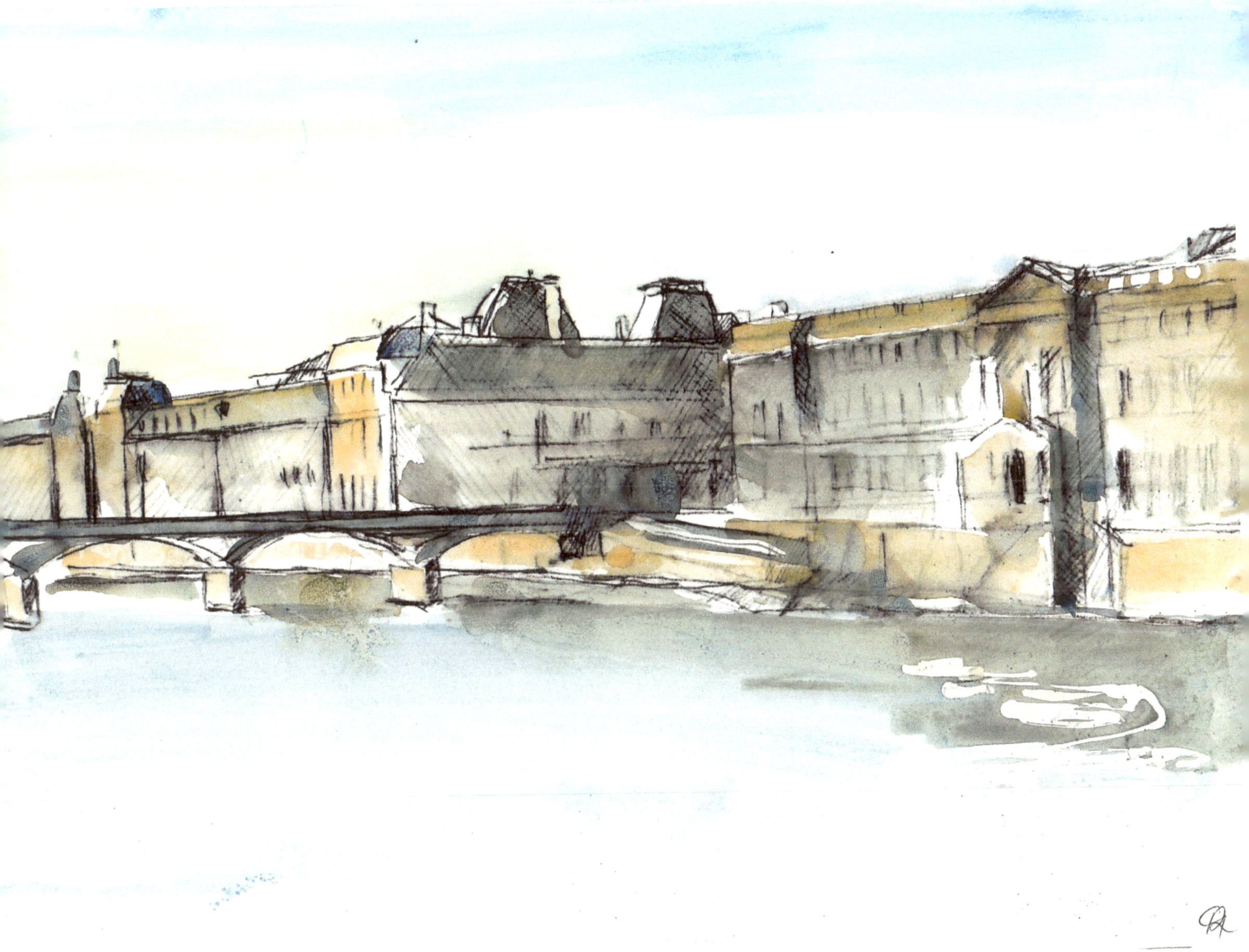

CHARLES BAUDELAIRE

These curses, these laments, these blasphemies,
These sobs, these shrieks, these Te Deums, these ecstasies
Are one echo ringing off a thousand labyrinth walls;
The divine opium of the hearts of mortals.

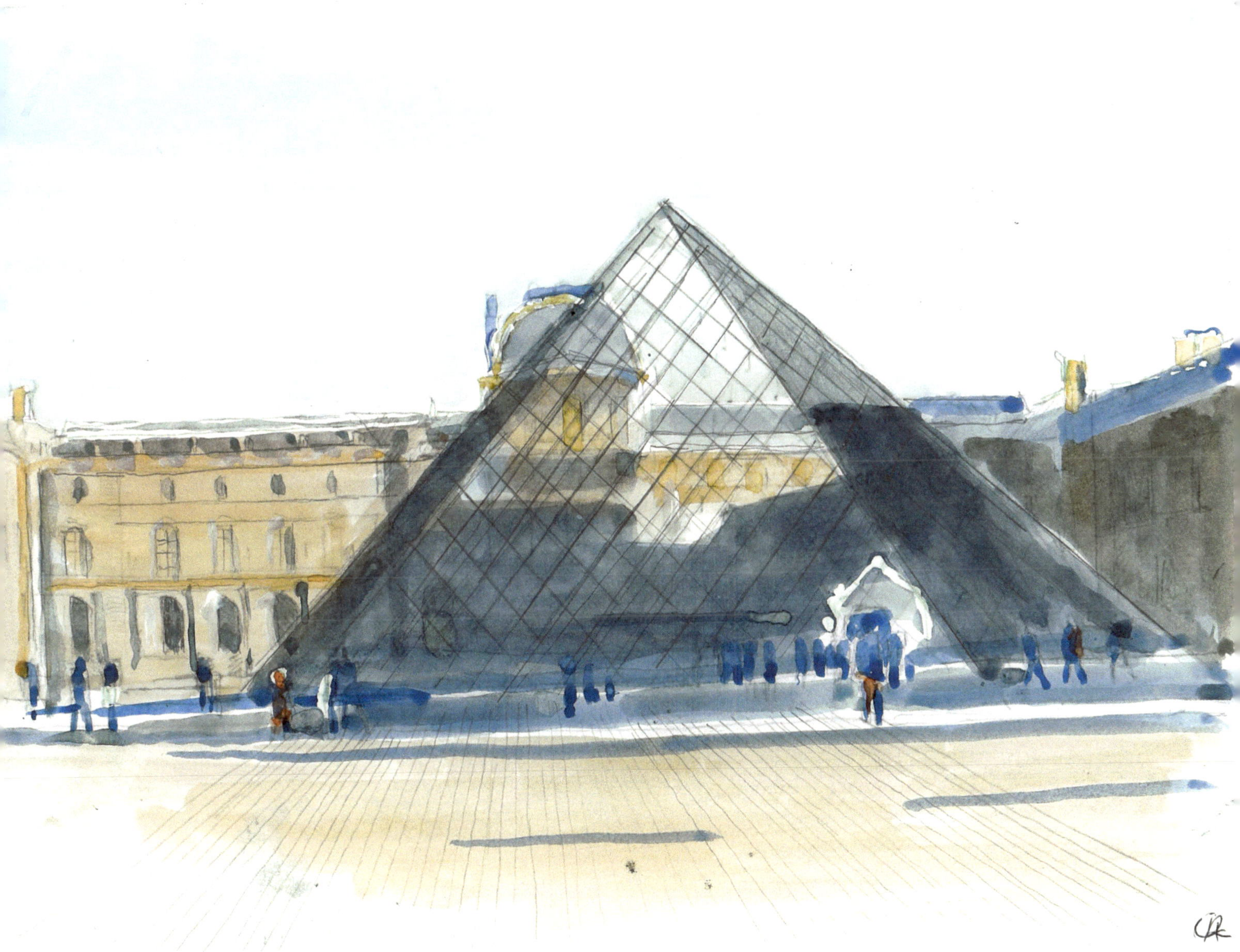

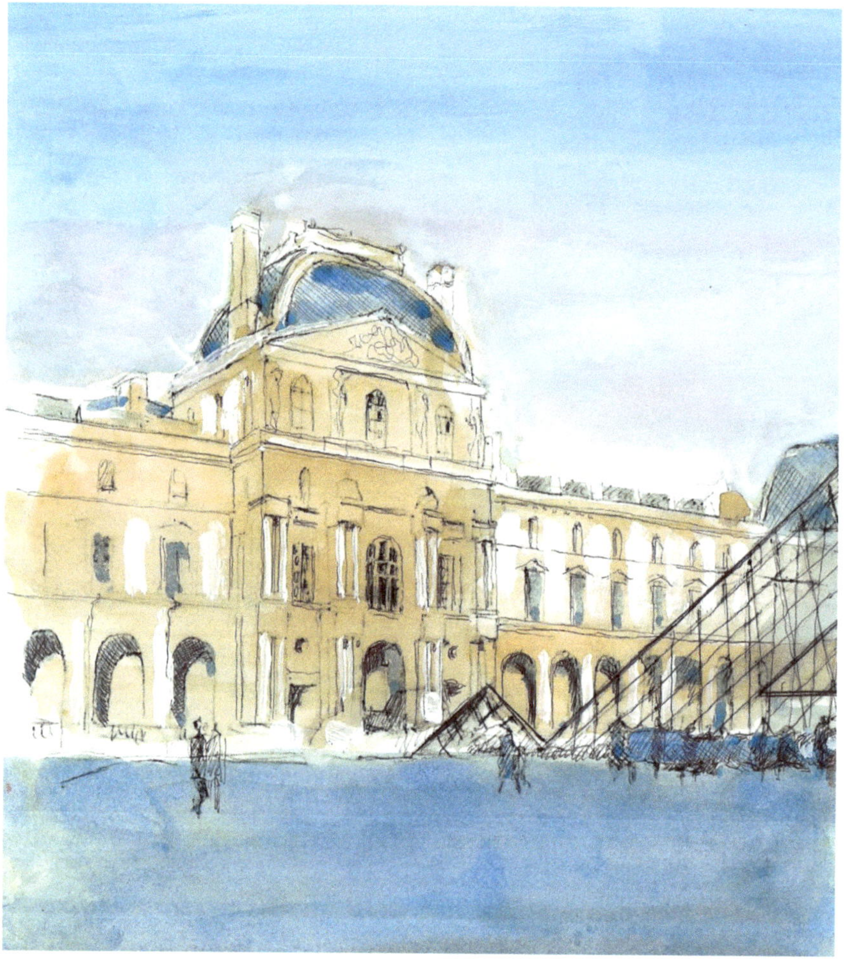

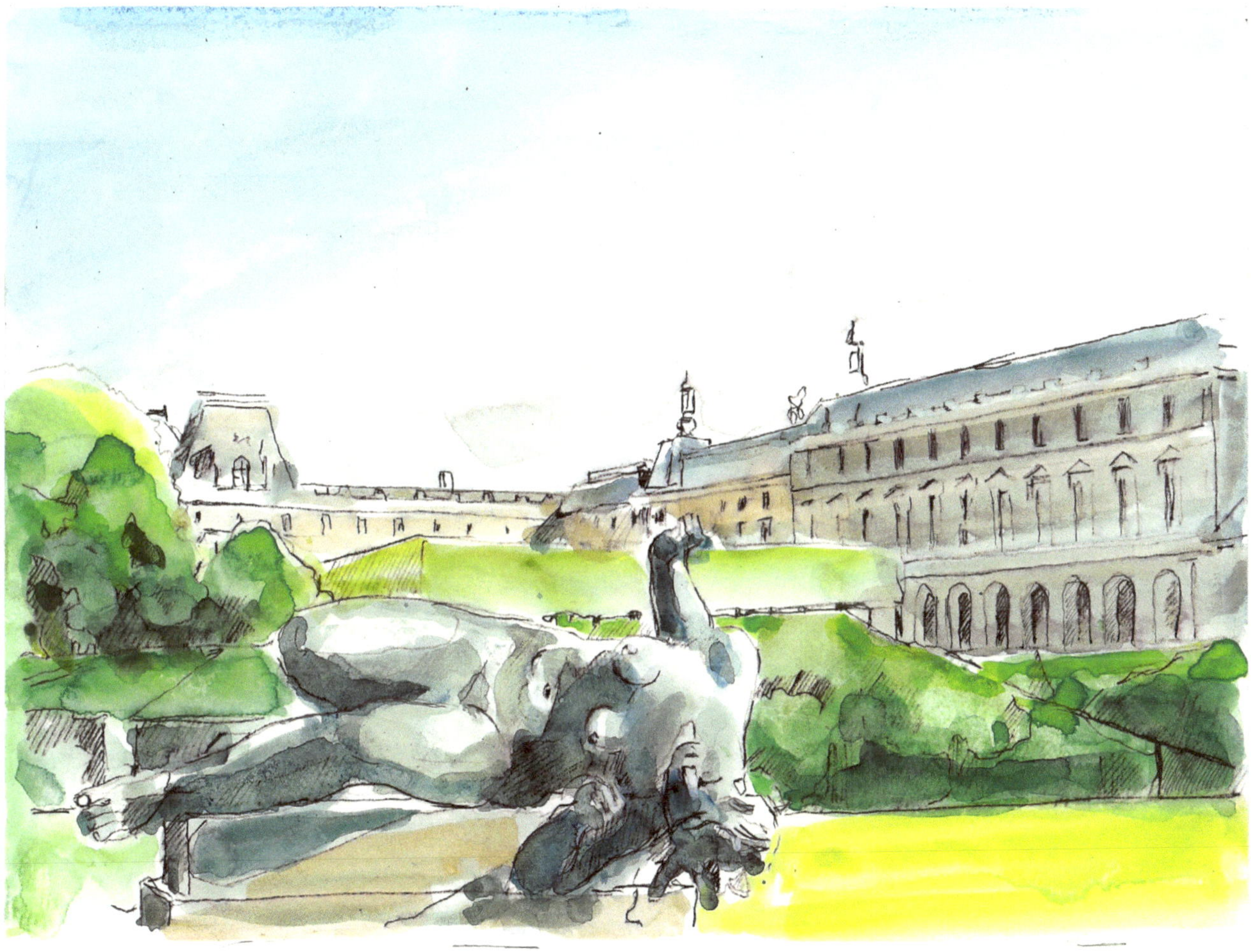

JULIAN BARNES

I walked to the Palais Royal feeling impressed with myself. I sat on a bench in the courtyard and inhaled the warm night. I felt as if everything was coming together, all at once. The past was all around: it was the present; art was there, and history, and now the promise of something much like love or sex. Over there in that corner was where Molière worked; across there, Cocteau, then Colette; there Blücher lost six million at roulette and for the rest of his life flew into a rage when the name of Paris was mentioned; there the first *café méchanique* was open; and there, over there, at a little cutler's in the Galerie de Valois, Charlotte Corday bought the knife with which she killed Marat. And bringing it all together, ingesting it, making it mine, was me – fusing all the art and the history with what I might soon, with luck, be calling life.

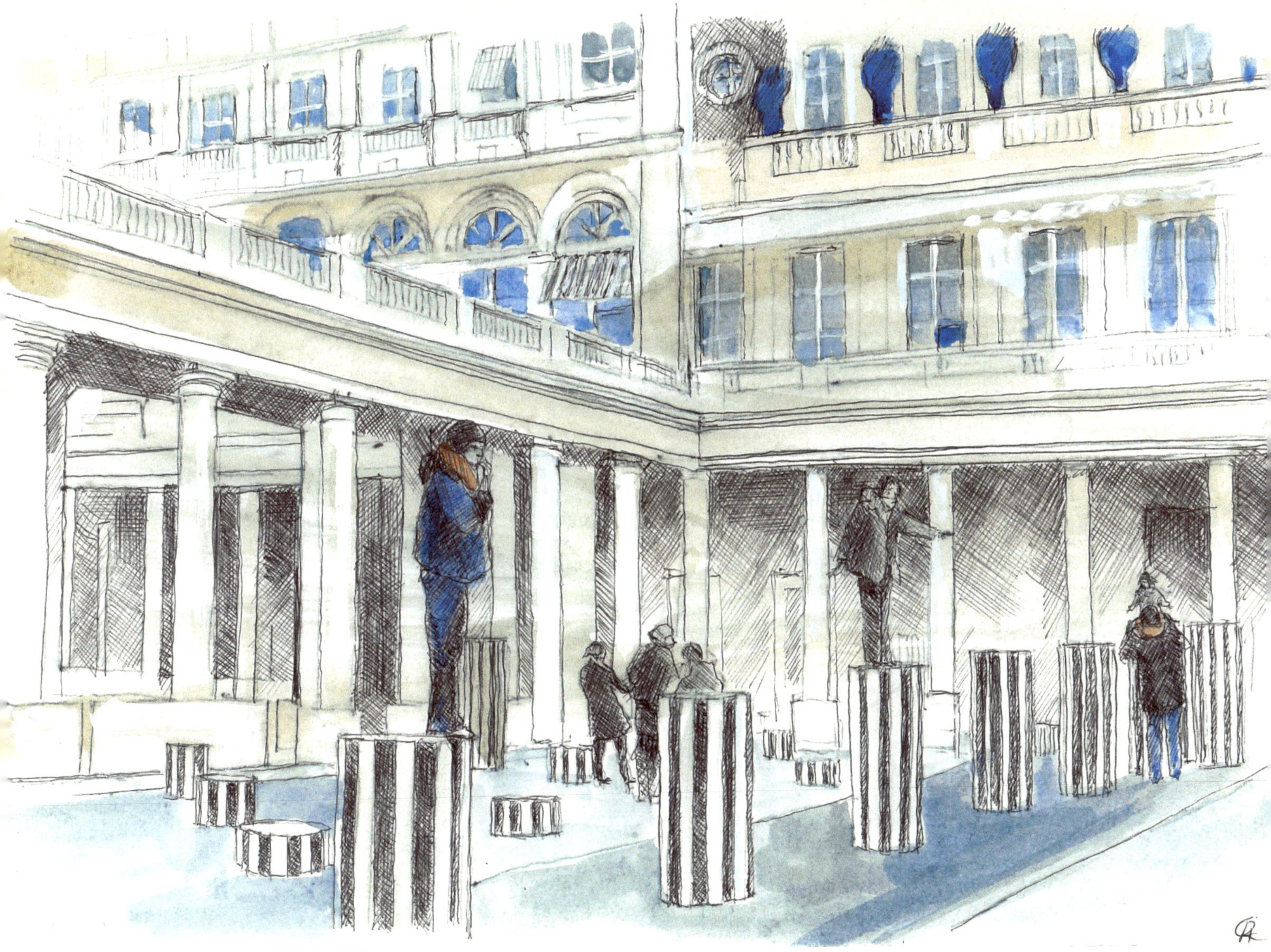

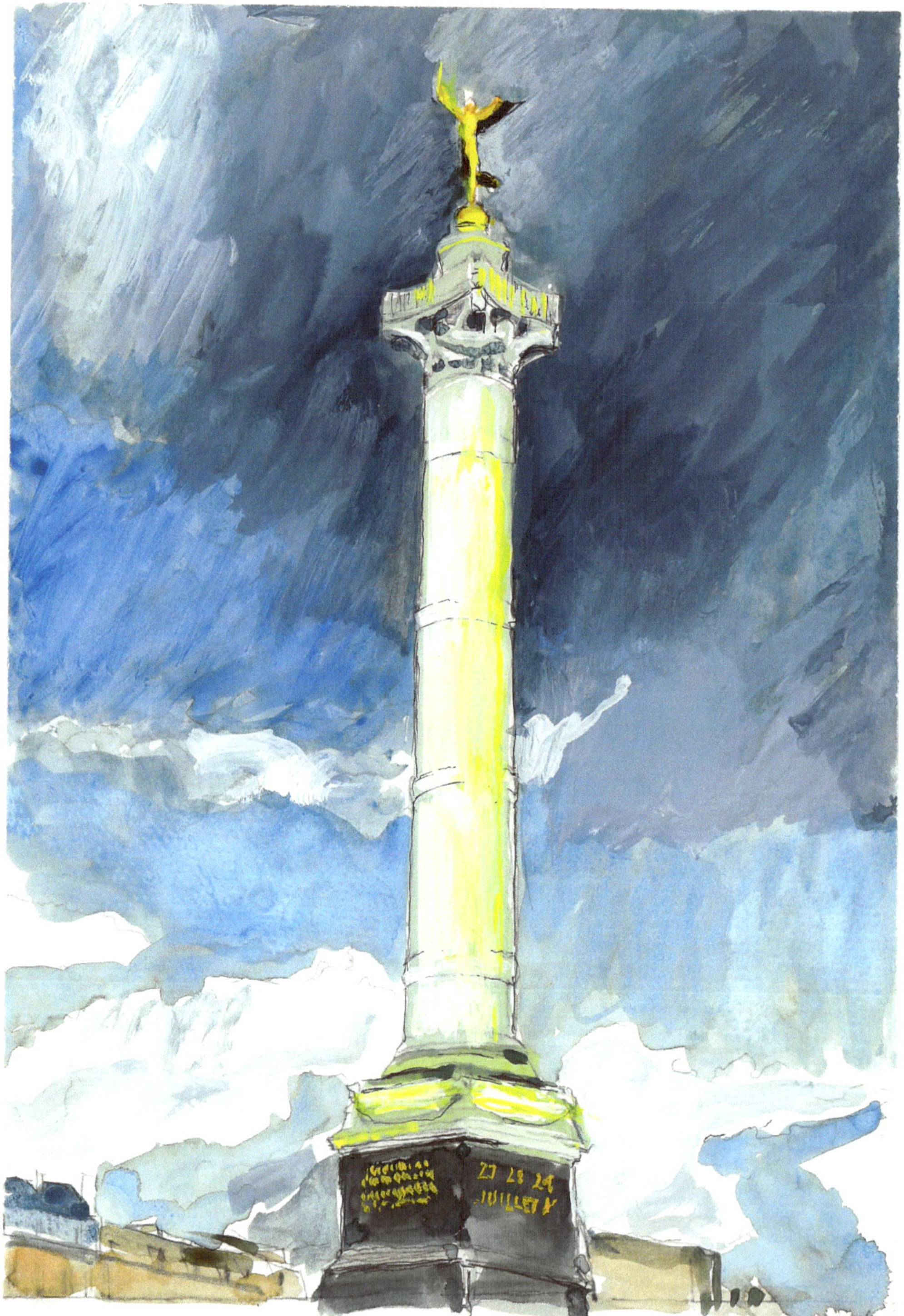

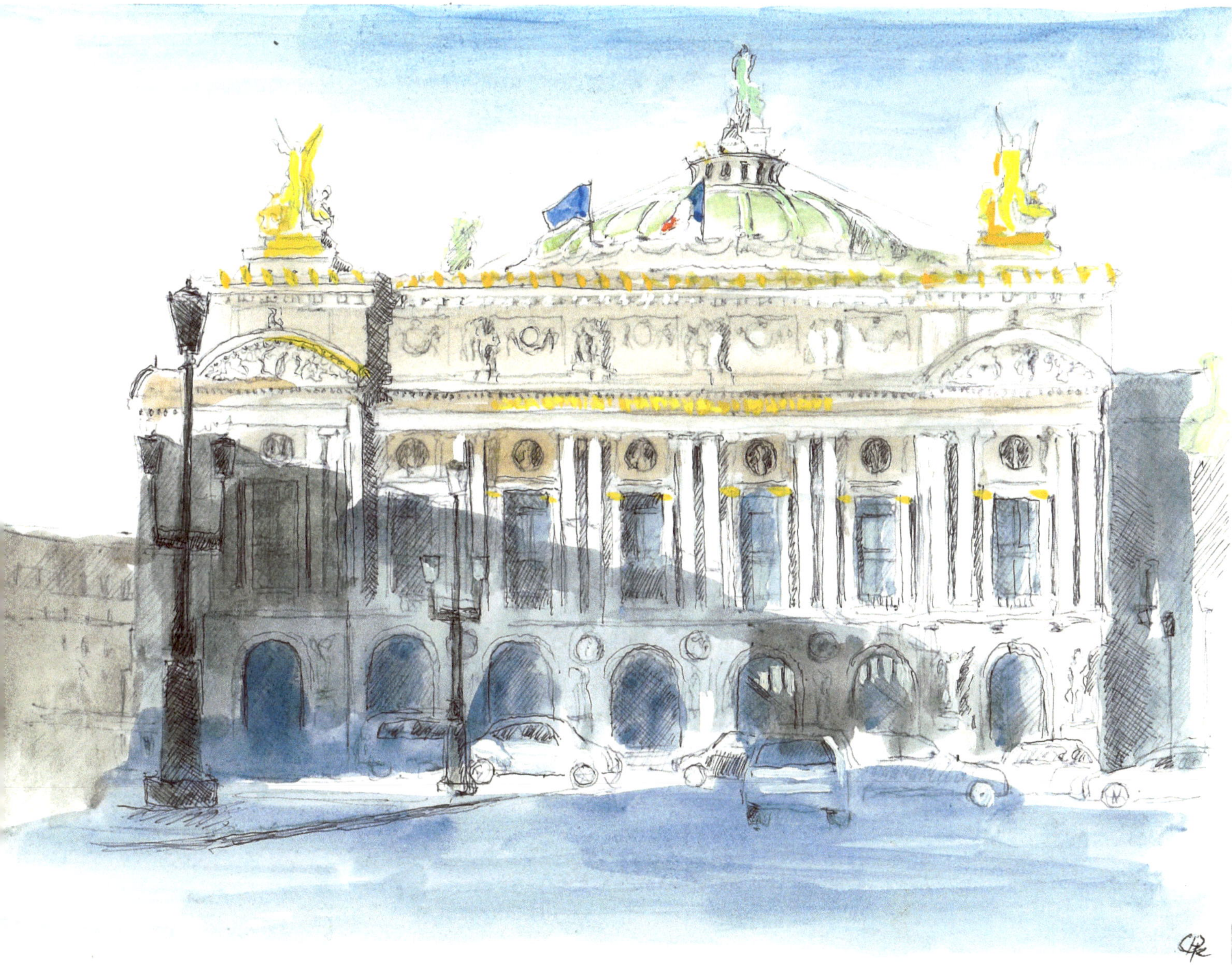

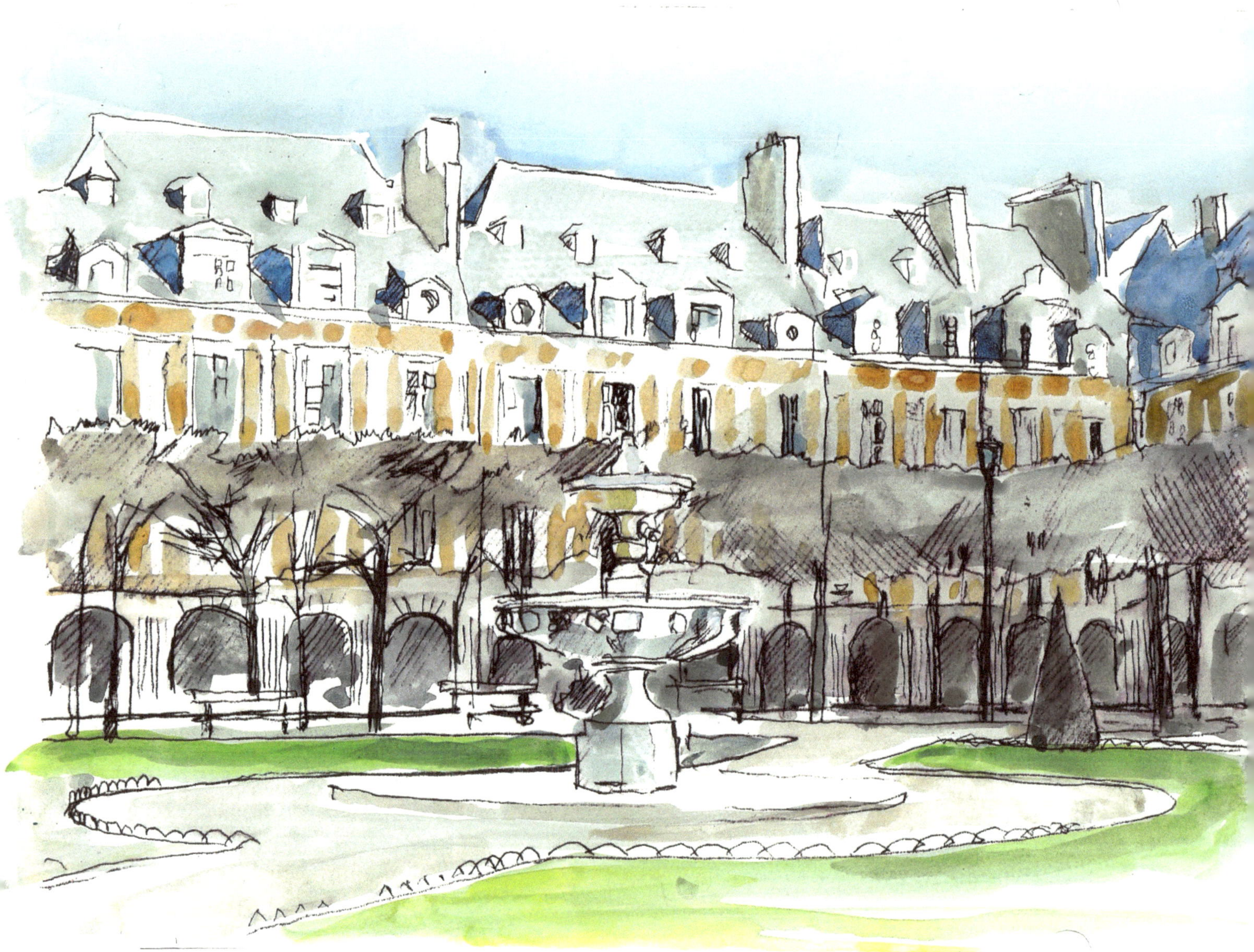

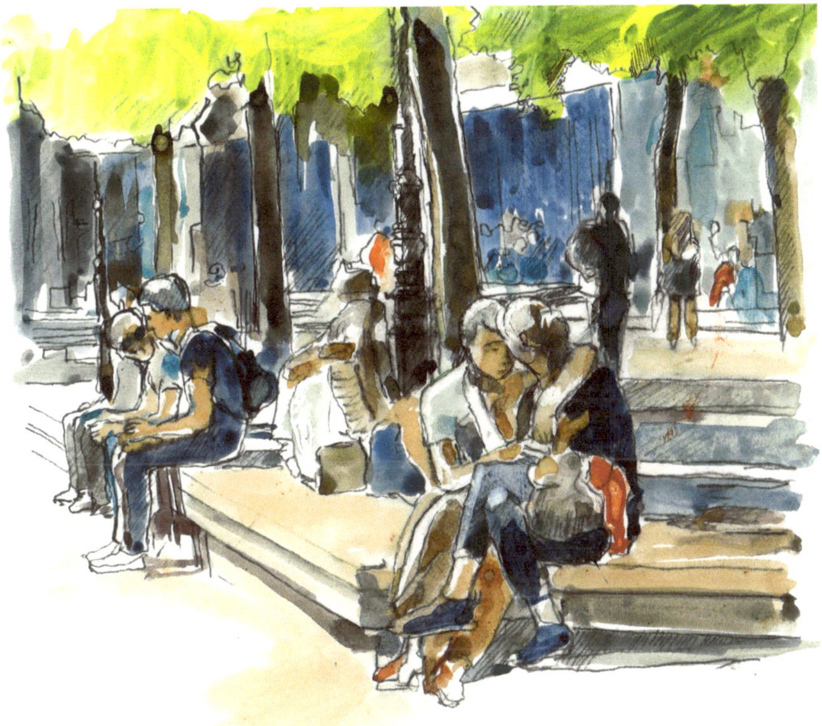

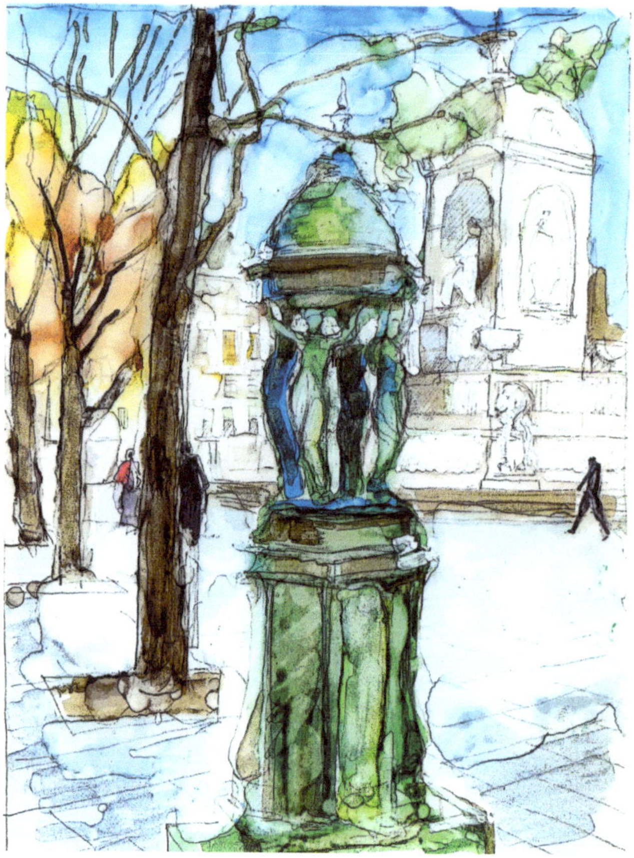

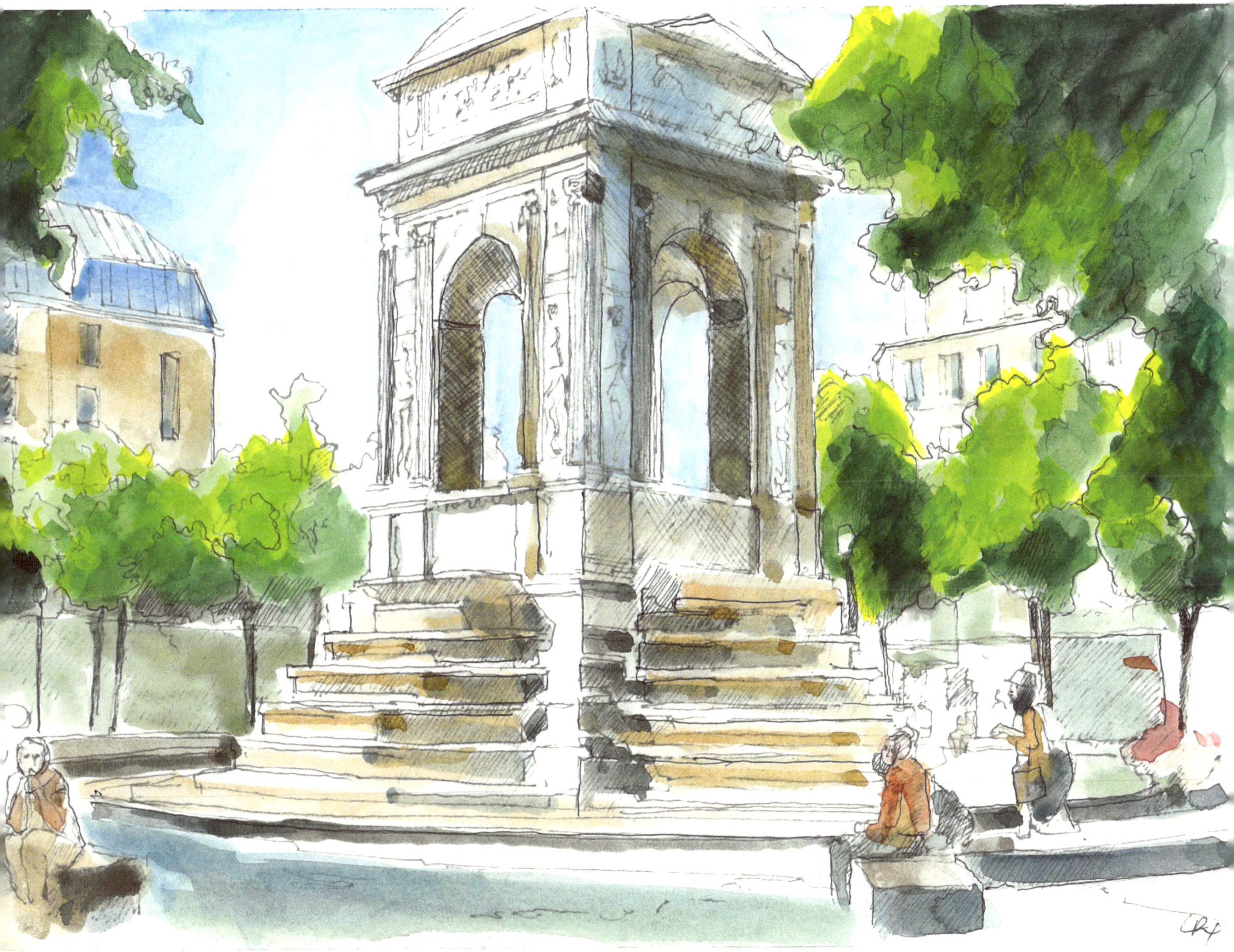

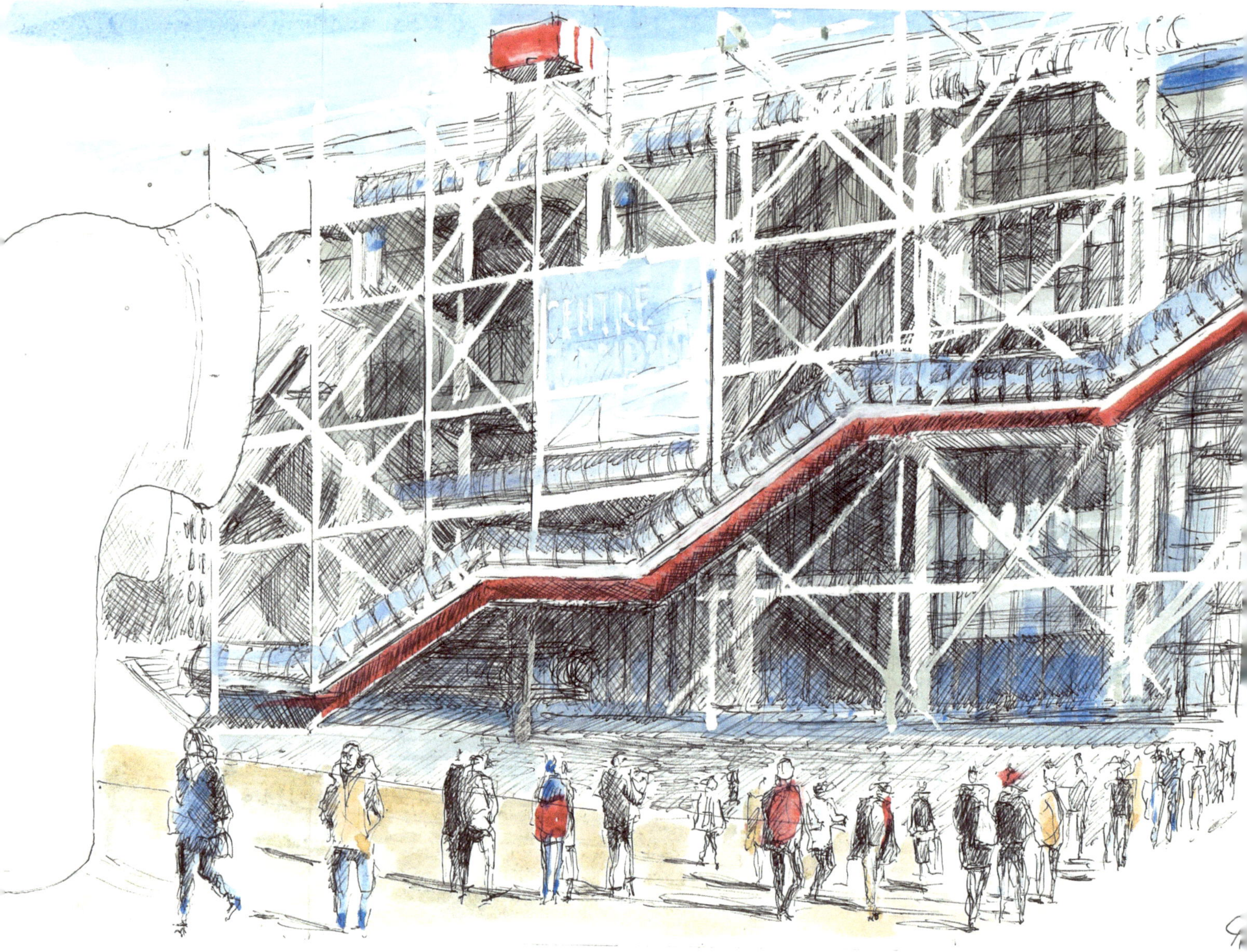
CENTRE

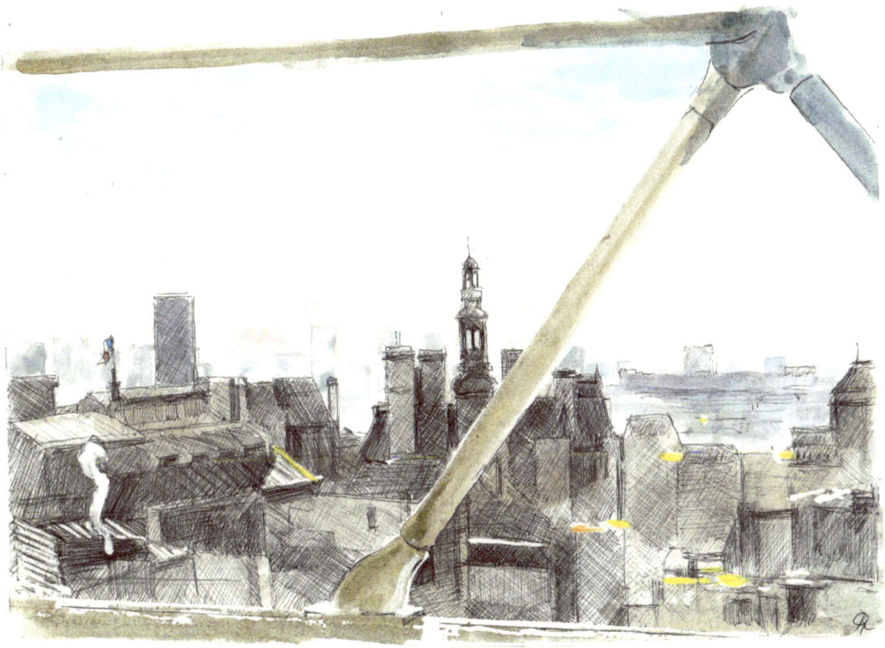

MARINA TSVETAEVA

Roofs reach the stars, the sky is low,
And closer to the earth, its vapour thronging
In Paris, so large, so full of joy,
Still the old secret longing.

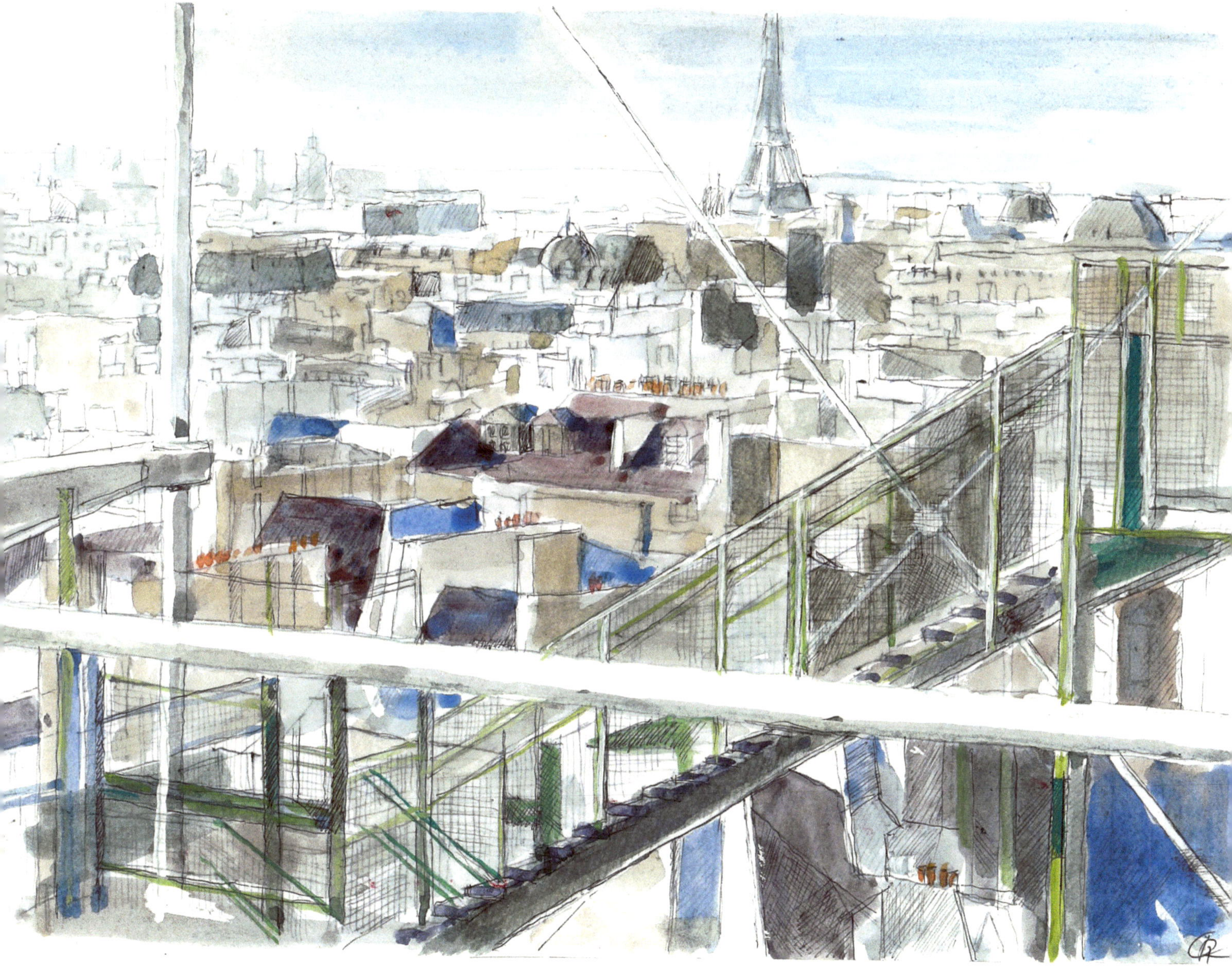

ANNE RICE

Paris was a universe whole and entire unto herself, hollowed and fashioned by history; so she seemed in this age of Napoleon III with her towering buildings, her massive cathedrals, her grand boulevards and ancient winding medieval streets – as vast and indestructible as nature itself. All was embraced by her, by her volatile and enchanted populace thronging the galleries, the theaters, the cafés, giving birth over and over to genius and sanctity, philosophy and war, frivolity and the finest art; so it seemed that if all the world outside her were to sink into darkness, what was fine, what was beautiful, what was essential might there still come to its finest flower. Even the majestic trees that graced and sheltered her streets were attuned to her – and the waters of the Seine, contained and beautiful as they wound through her heart; so that the earth on that spot, so shaped by blood and consciousness, had ceased to be the earth
and had become Paris.

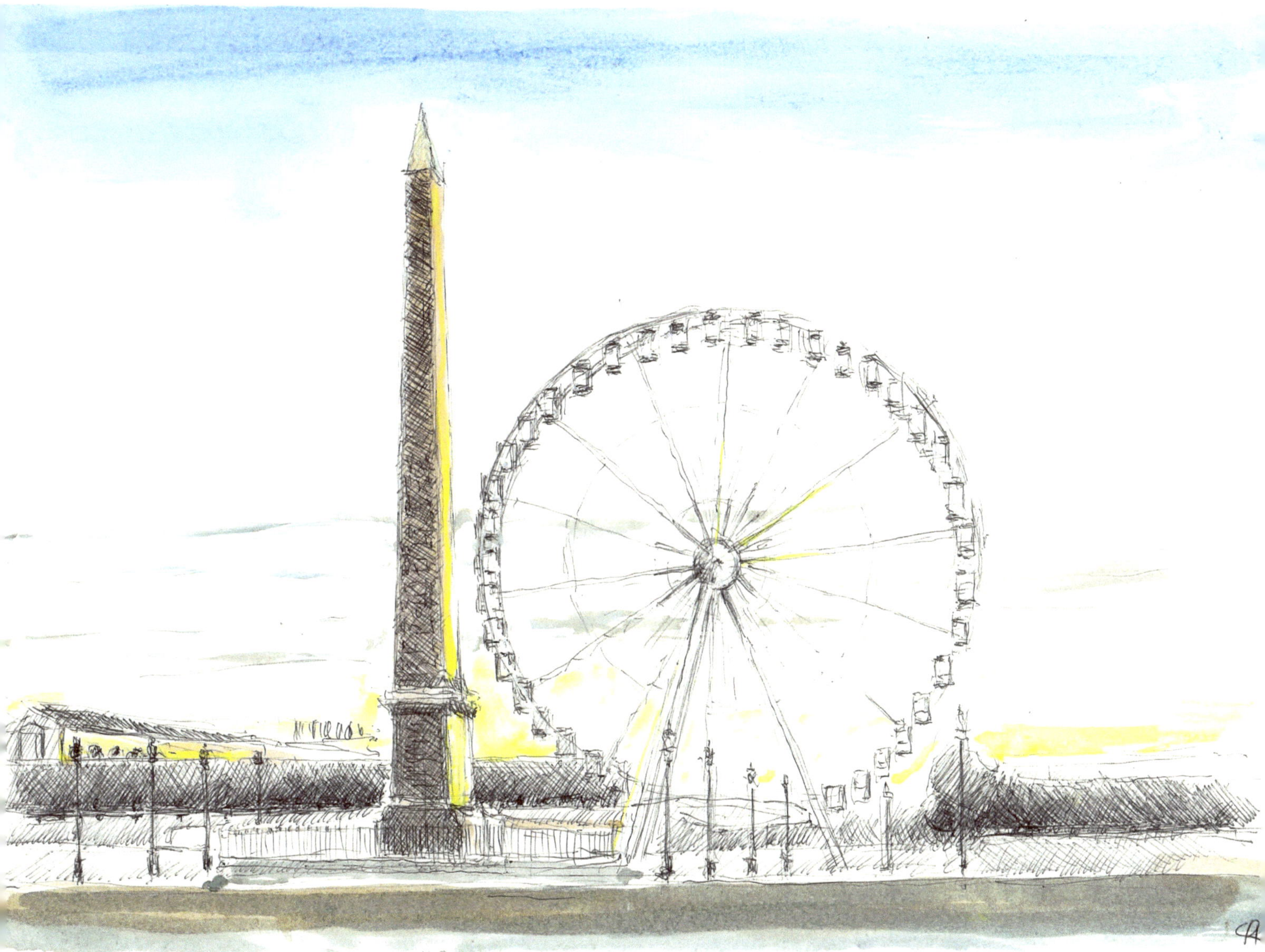

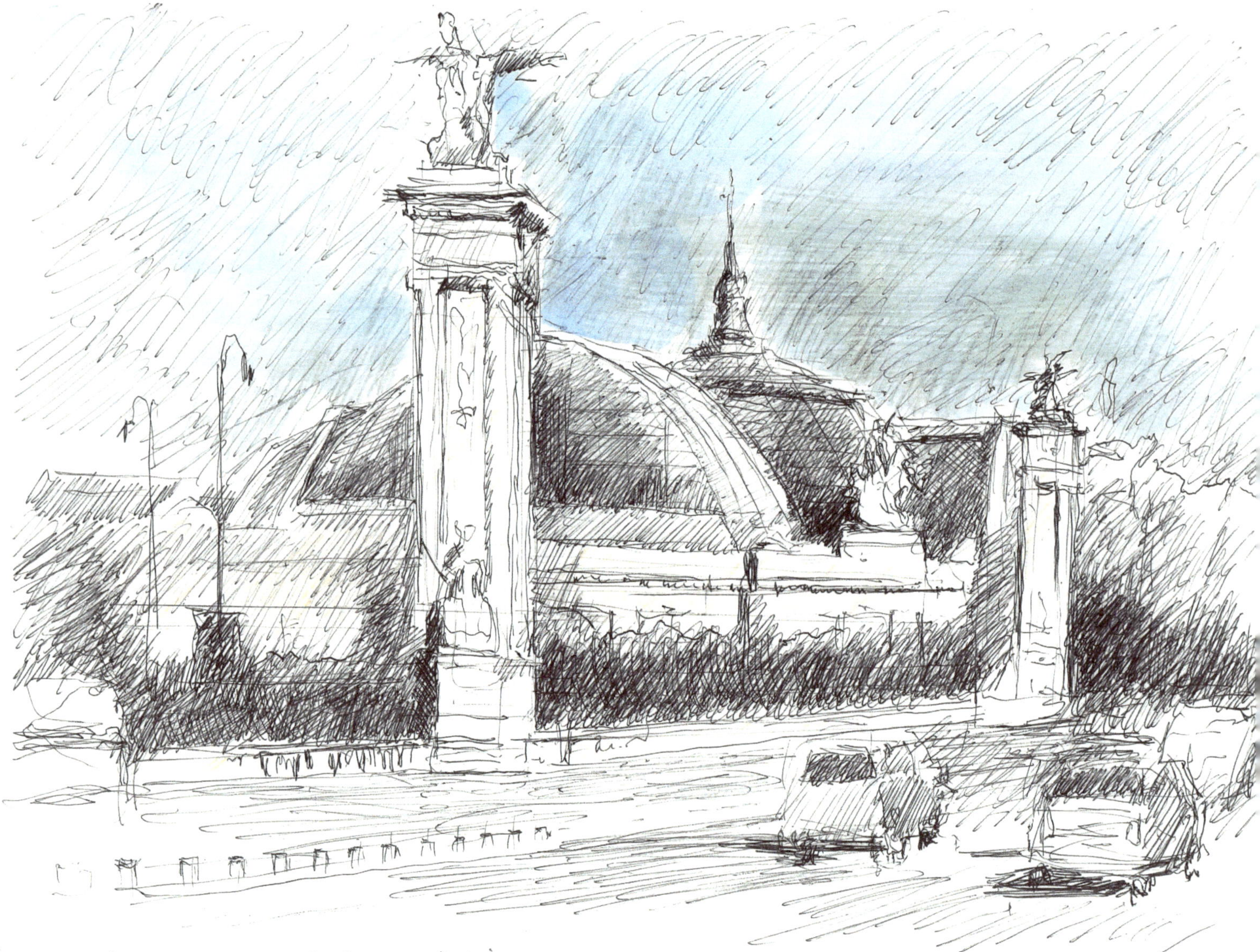

Le pont Alexandre III le Grand Palais

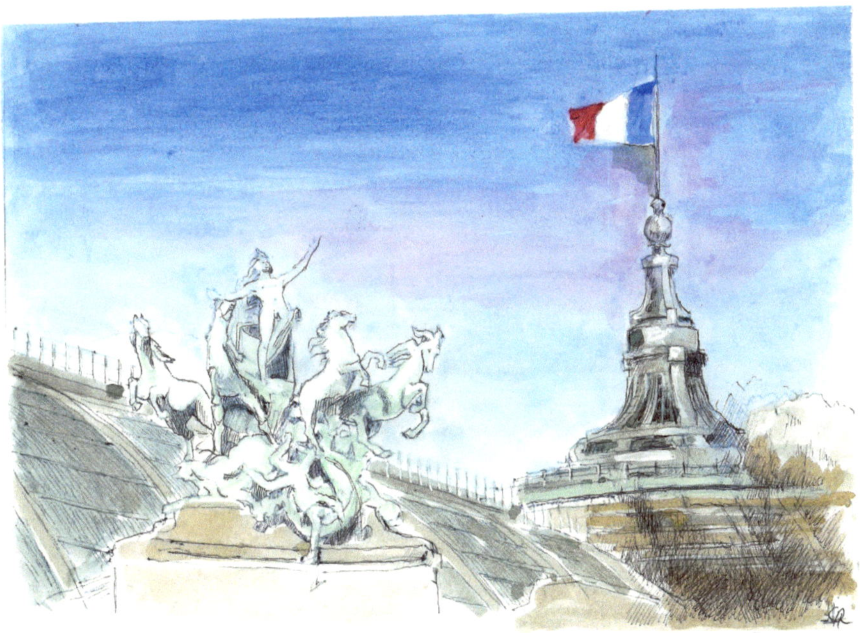

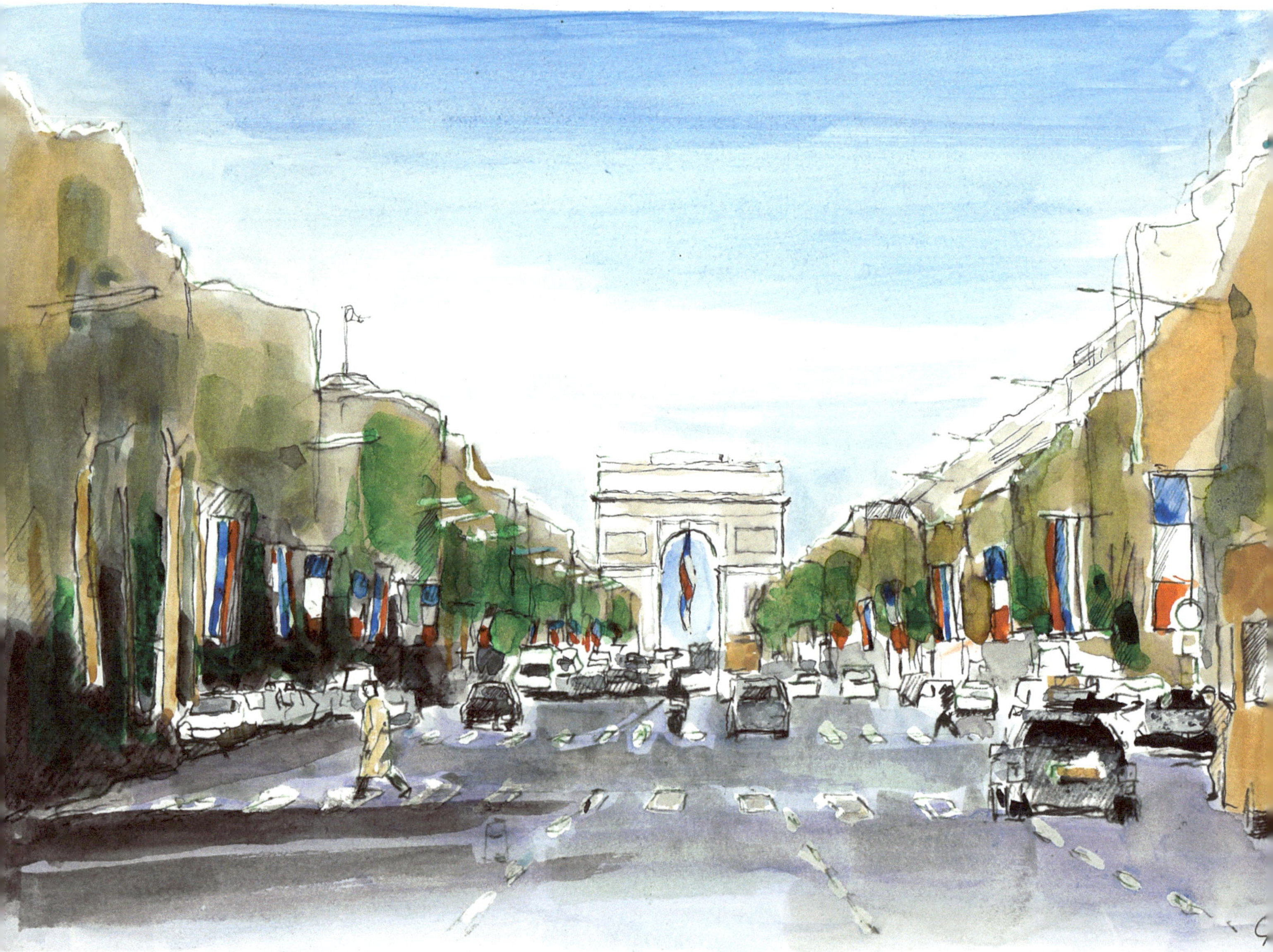

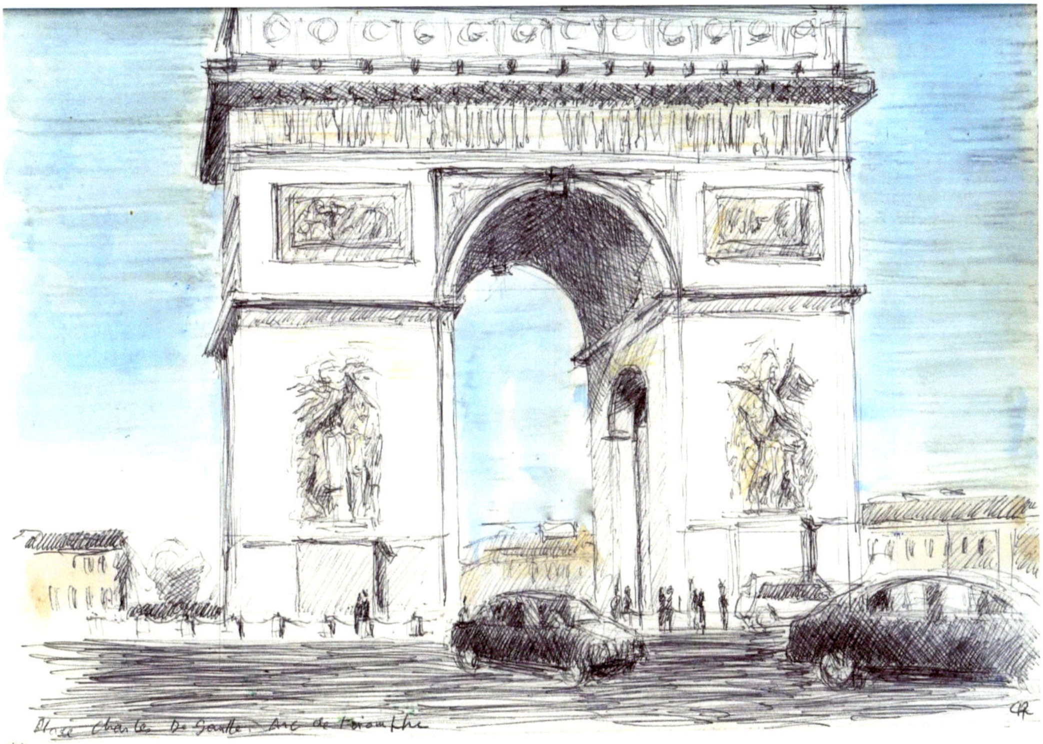

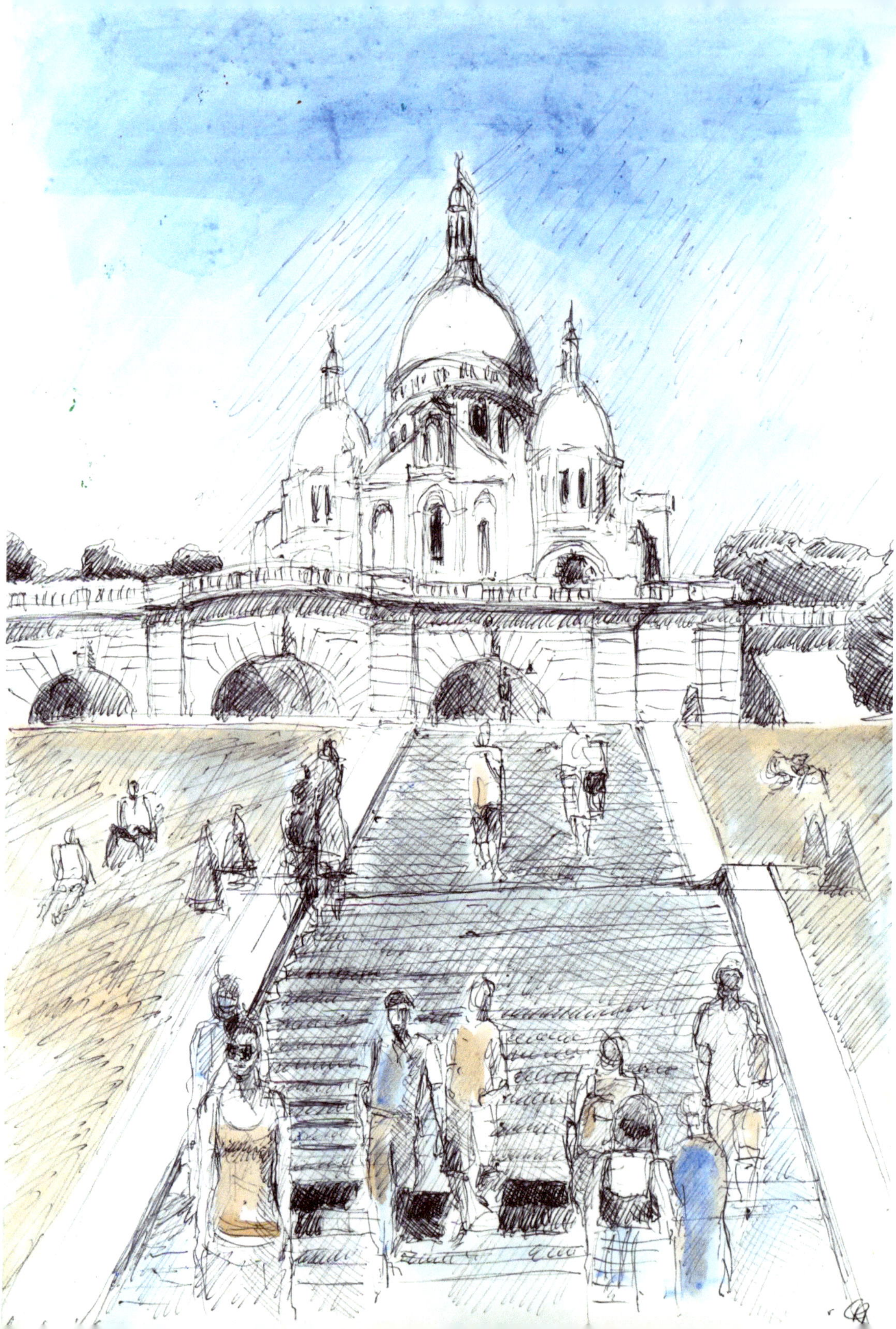

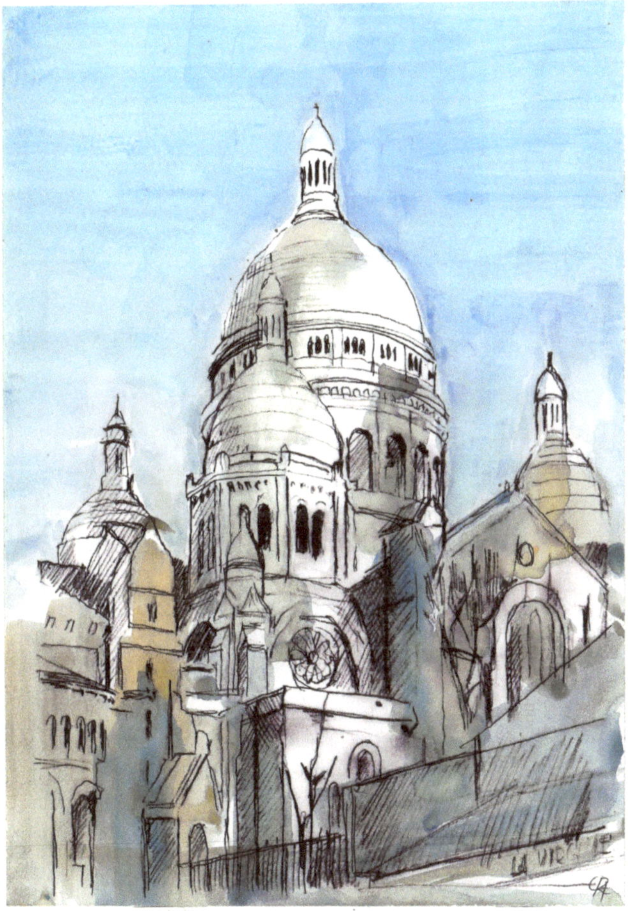

CHARLES BAUDELAIRE

I need to live among the roofs and towers
Like an astrologer among the stars,
I need to dream (to write my pastorals)
Through solemn noises from the nearby bells,
And wake, and hear them still; lean out and see
The many-masted city under me,
Paris, my restless workshop: drainpipes, spires,
The endless sky in reach of my desires.

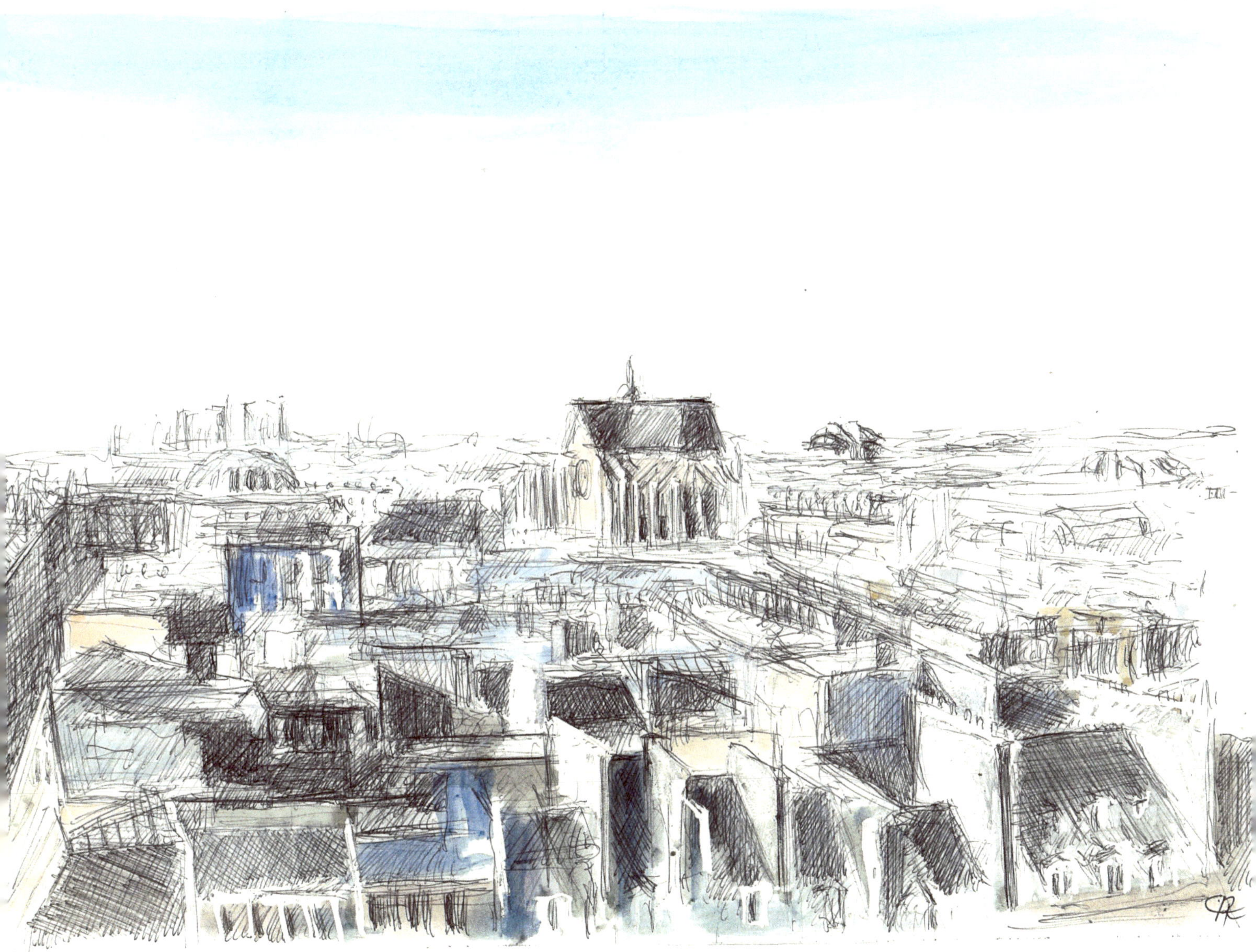

GERTRUDE STEIN

Gertrude and I about ten days later went to Montmartre, I for the first time. I have never ceased to love it. We go there every now and then and I always have the same tender expectant feeling that I had then.

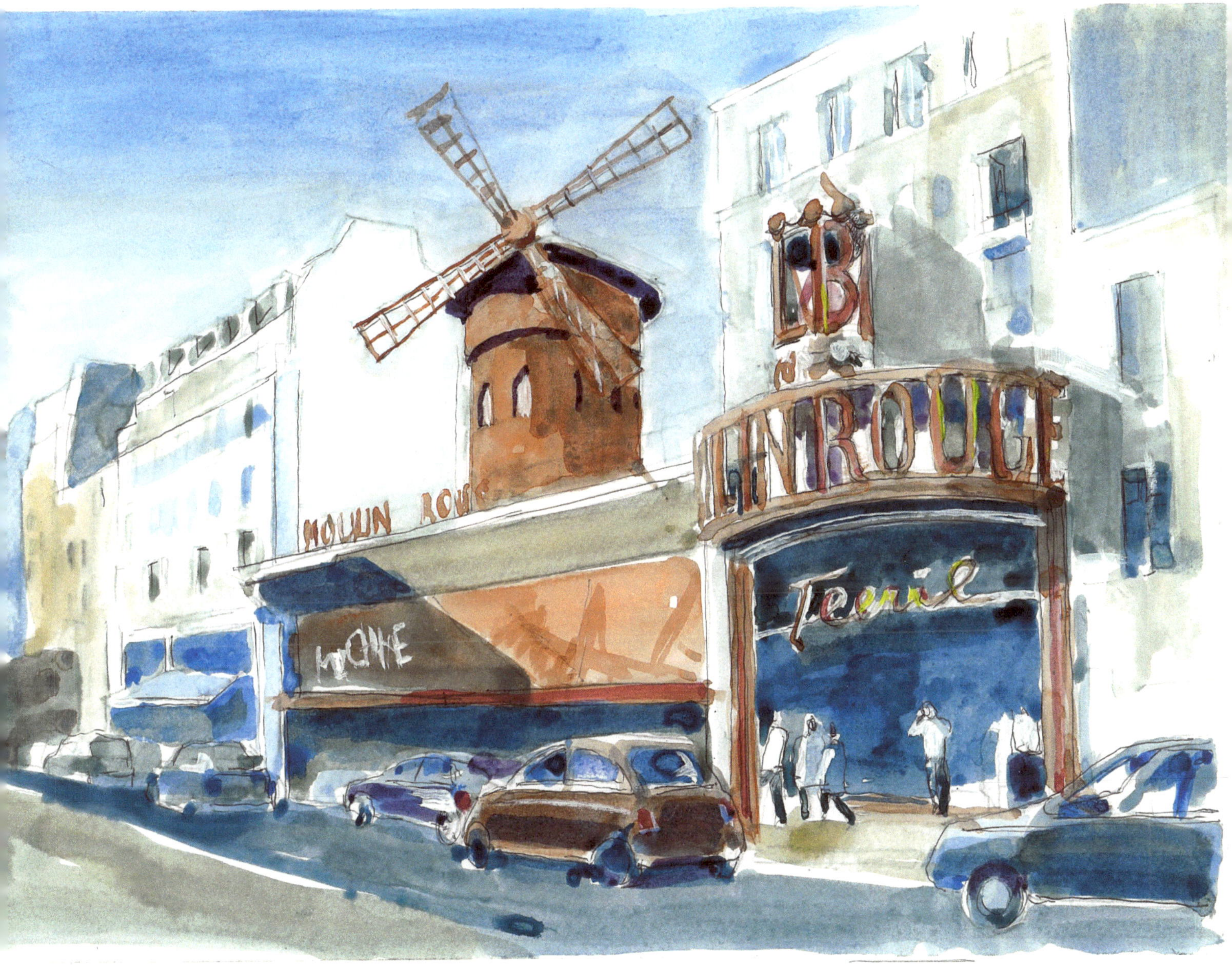

CHARLES BAUDELAIRE

Paris may change; my melancholy is fixed.

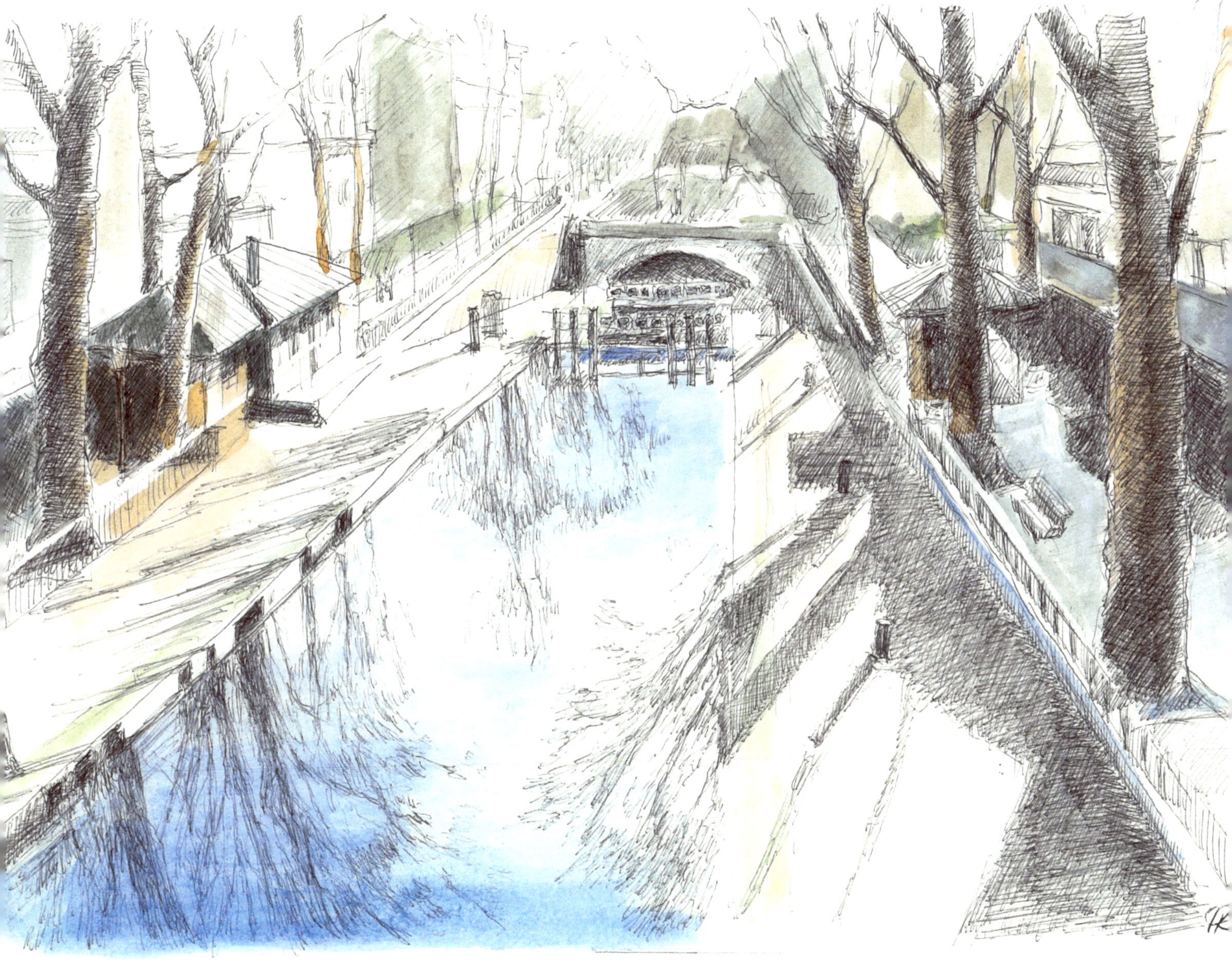

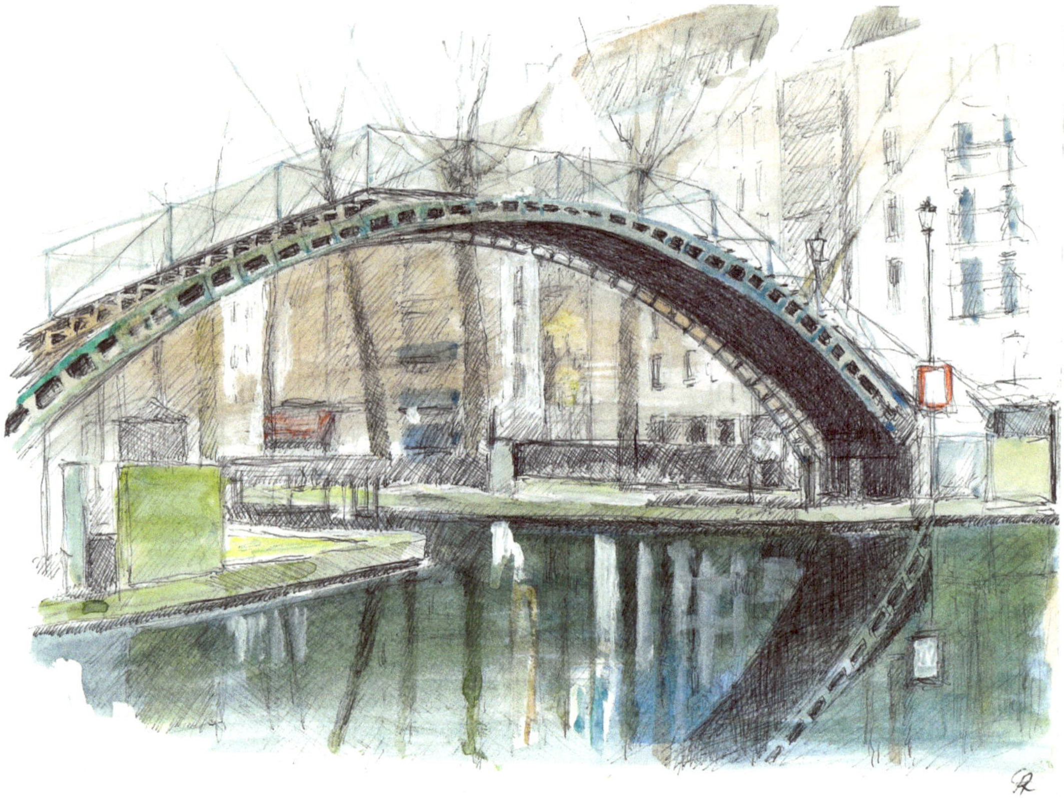

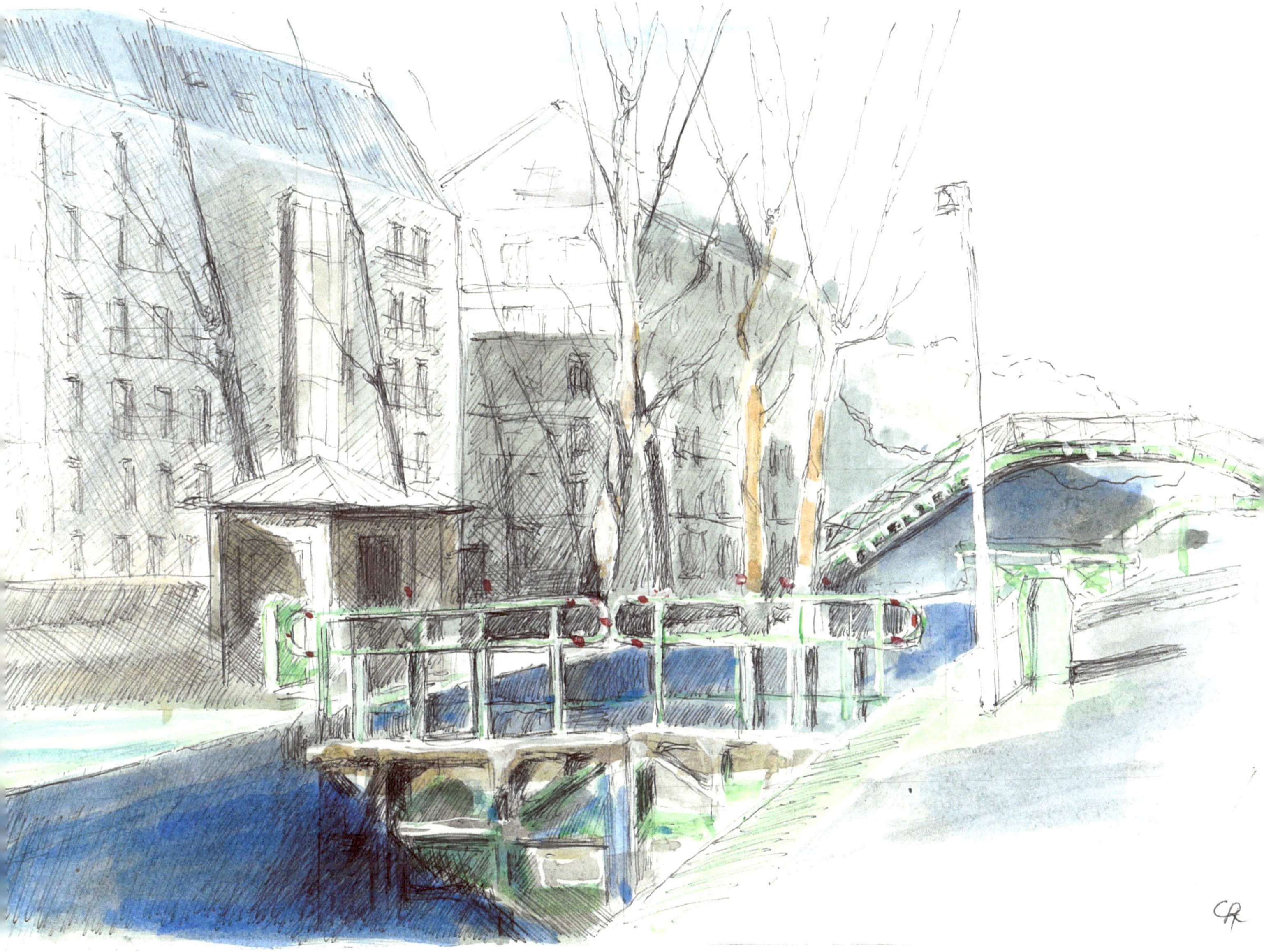

JACQUES BREL

Paris grey skies
The last day the last hour
Brings the first tear
Paris overcast
All the flowers have gone
From the garden we crossed

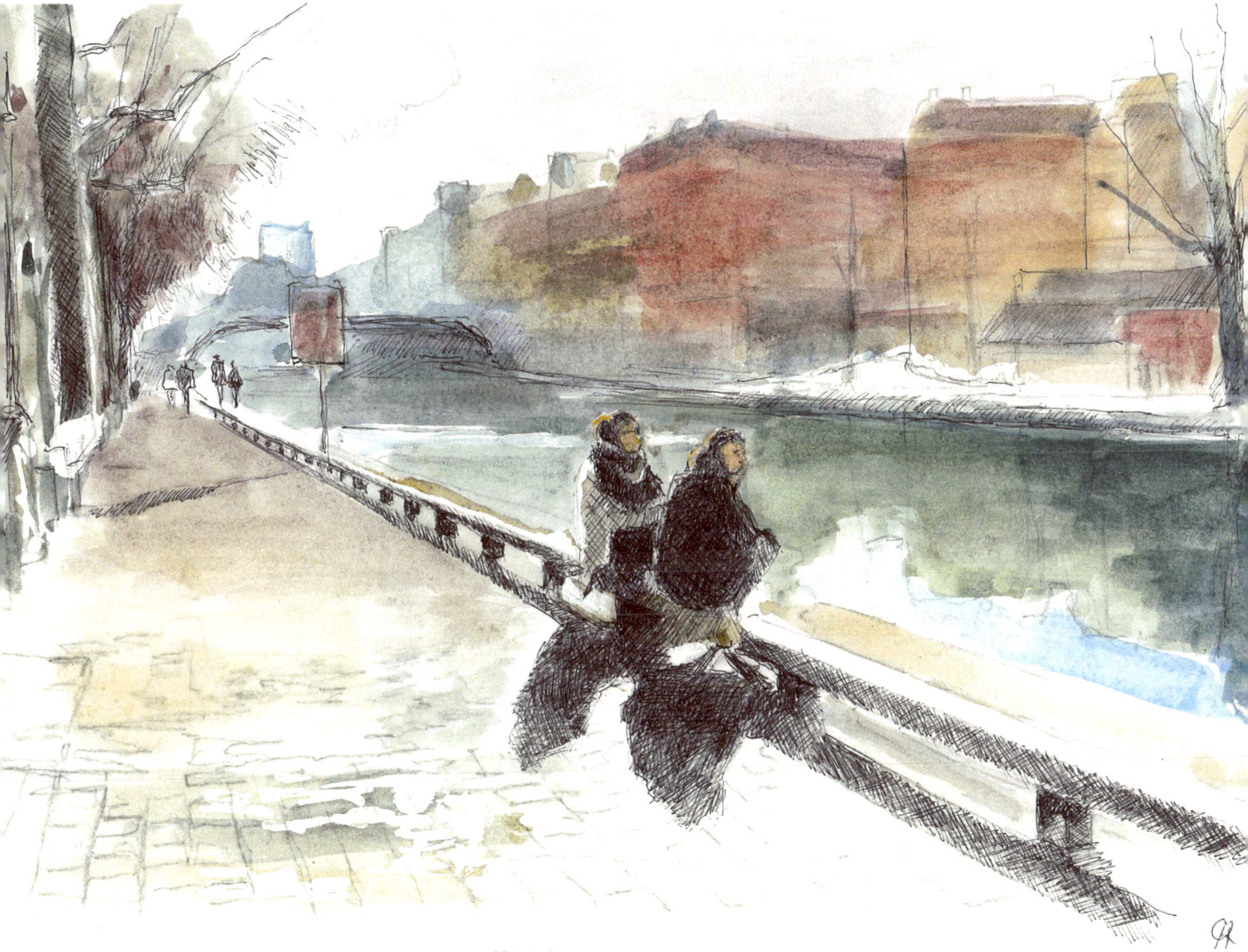

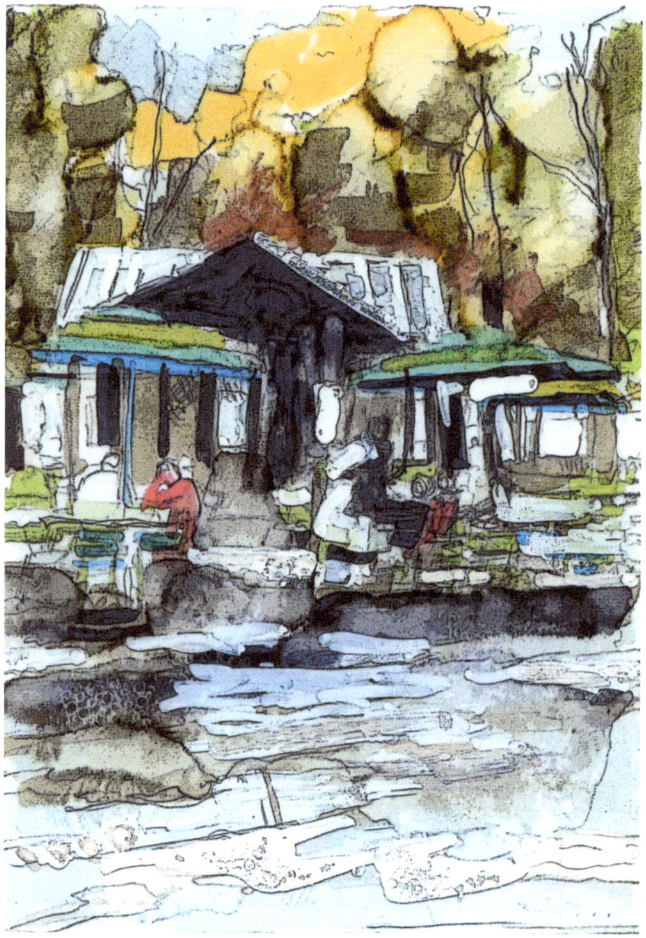

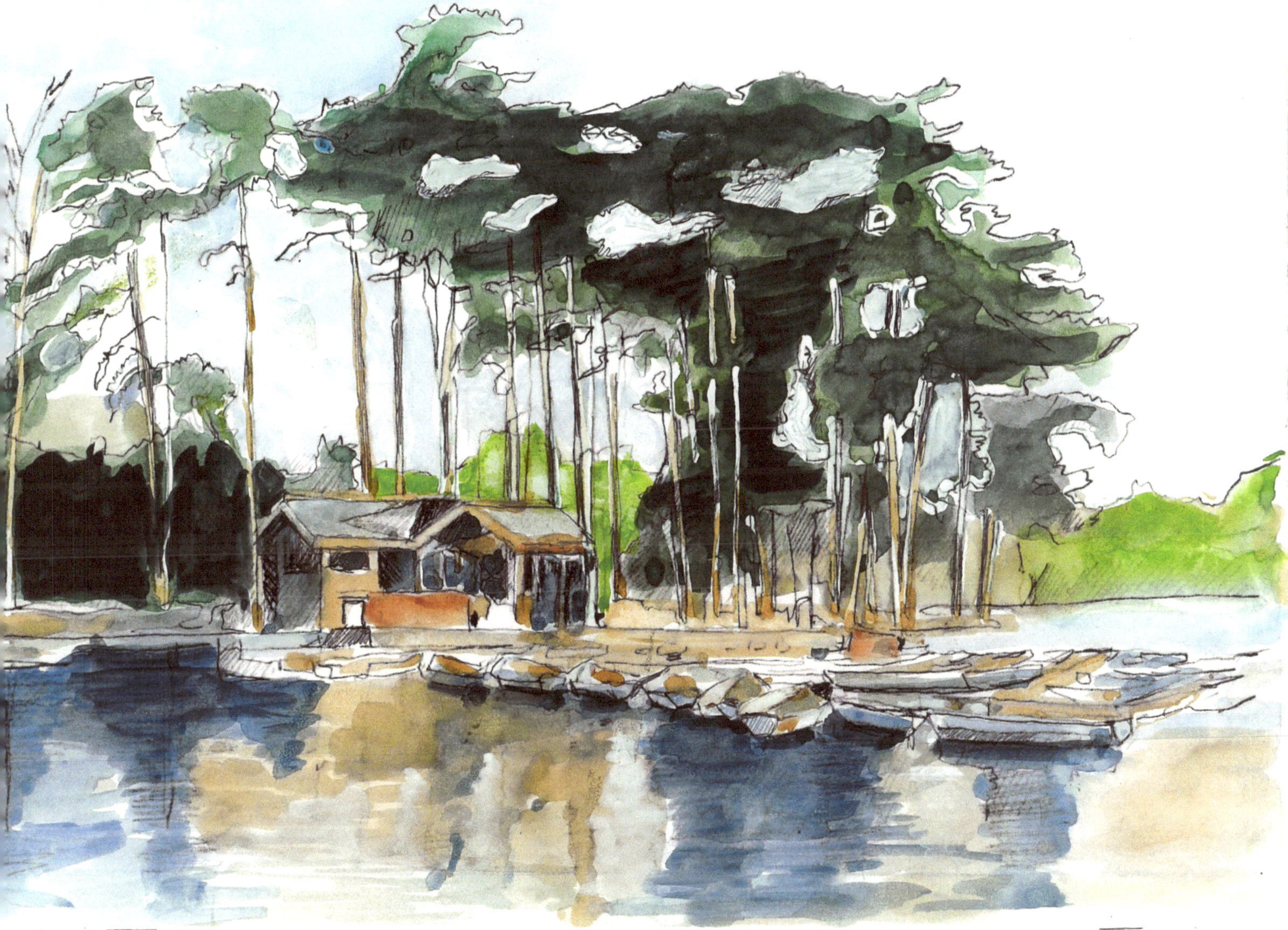

MARIE DARRIEUSSECQ

There are magnificent parks and gardens, as many cinemas as you could want, museums, shops, smart avenues, colourful neighbourhoods, and Parisians everywhere. I often walk around underneath the Tour Eiffel, between its four great arms. I head right for the middle, I look up and fall into the big hole that is the centre of the world. There are Japanese who come here for this reason alone; but afterwards they have to go and get on a plane and go an awful long way away. When I think all this has been put here for me, provincial girl that I was, I tell myself that life is beautiful, that the world is extremely well put together and that everything in it functions to perfection.

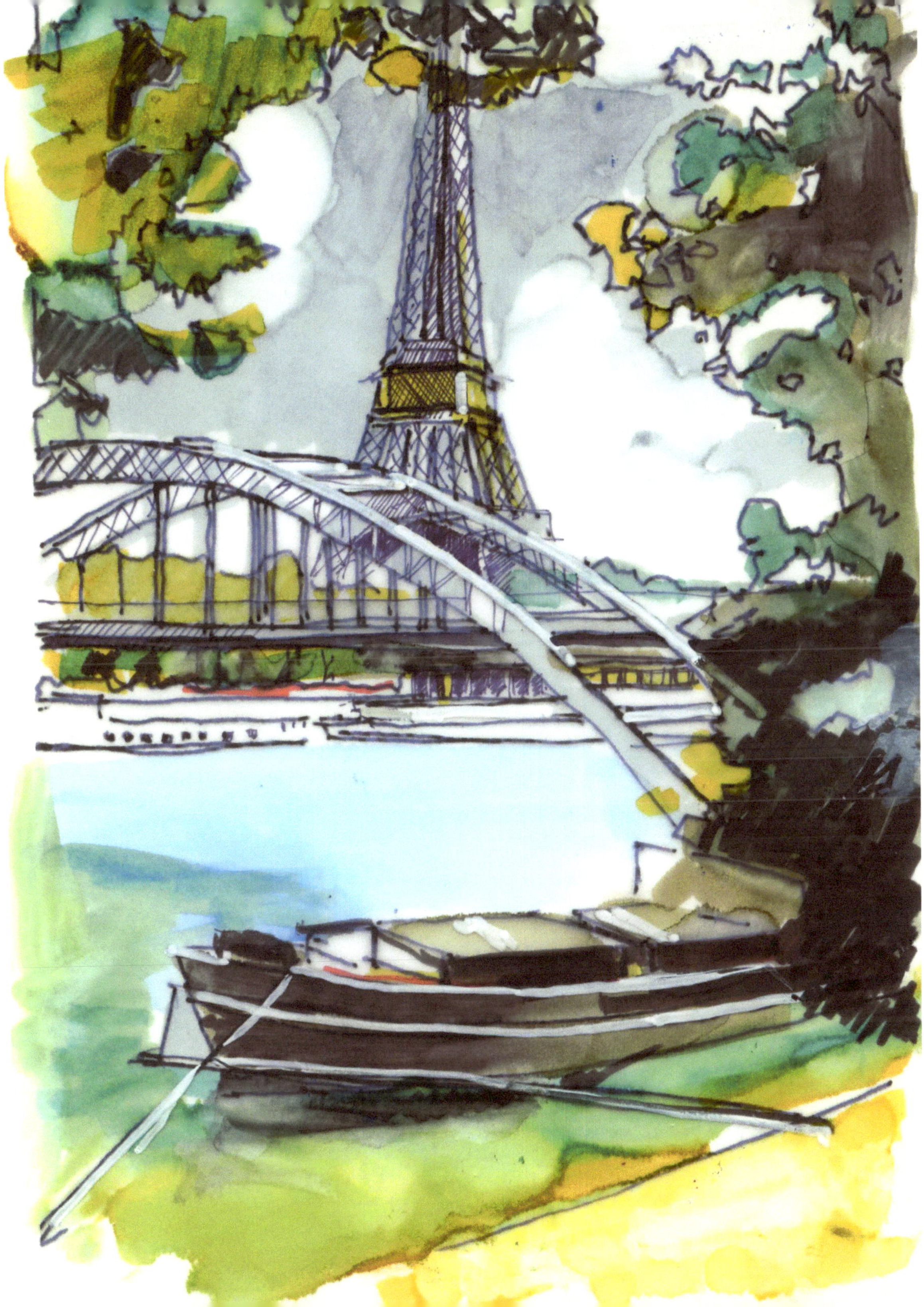

ANDRÉ FRÉNAUD

O sleeping ship
that waits for me
at a distance, o Paris
my honour and my feast,
my secret warmed
in your eyes.

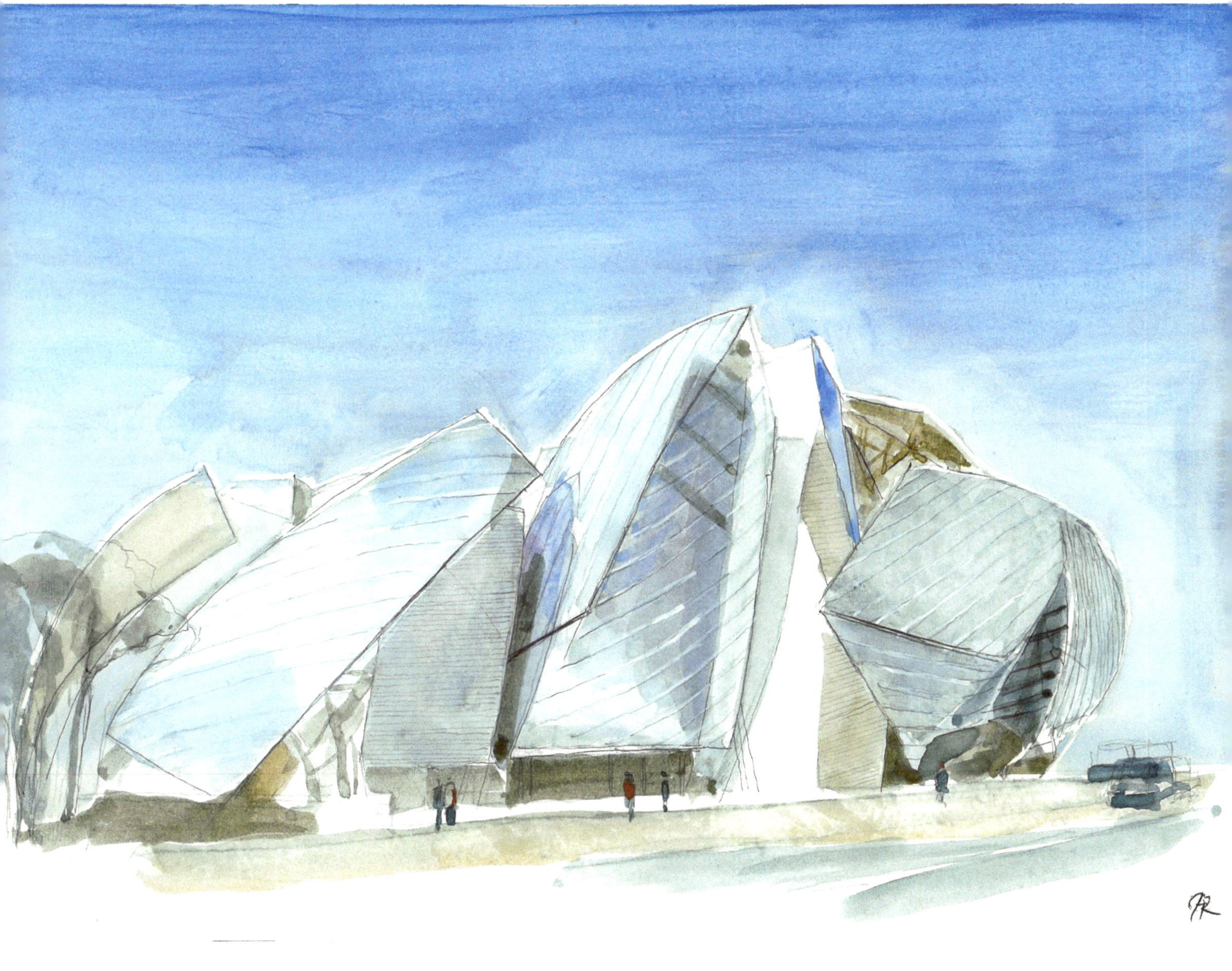

ERNEST HEMINGWAY

There is never any ending to Paris and the memory of each person who has lived in it differs from that of any other. We always returned to it no matter who we were or how it was changed or with what difficulties, or ease, it could be reached. Paris was always worth it and you received return for whatever you brought to it.

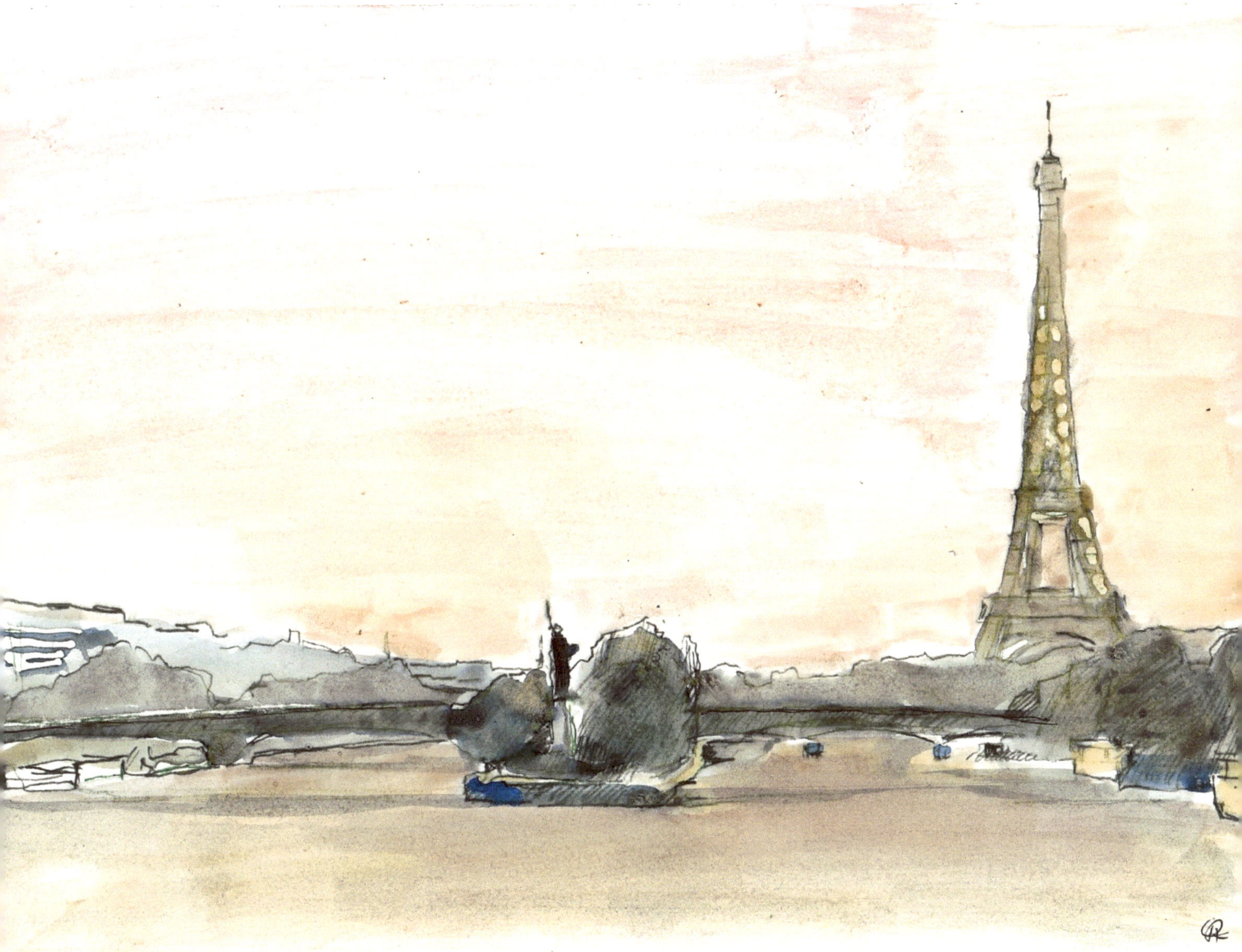

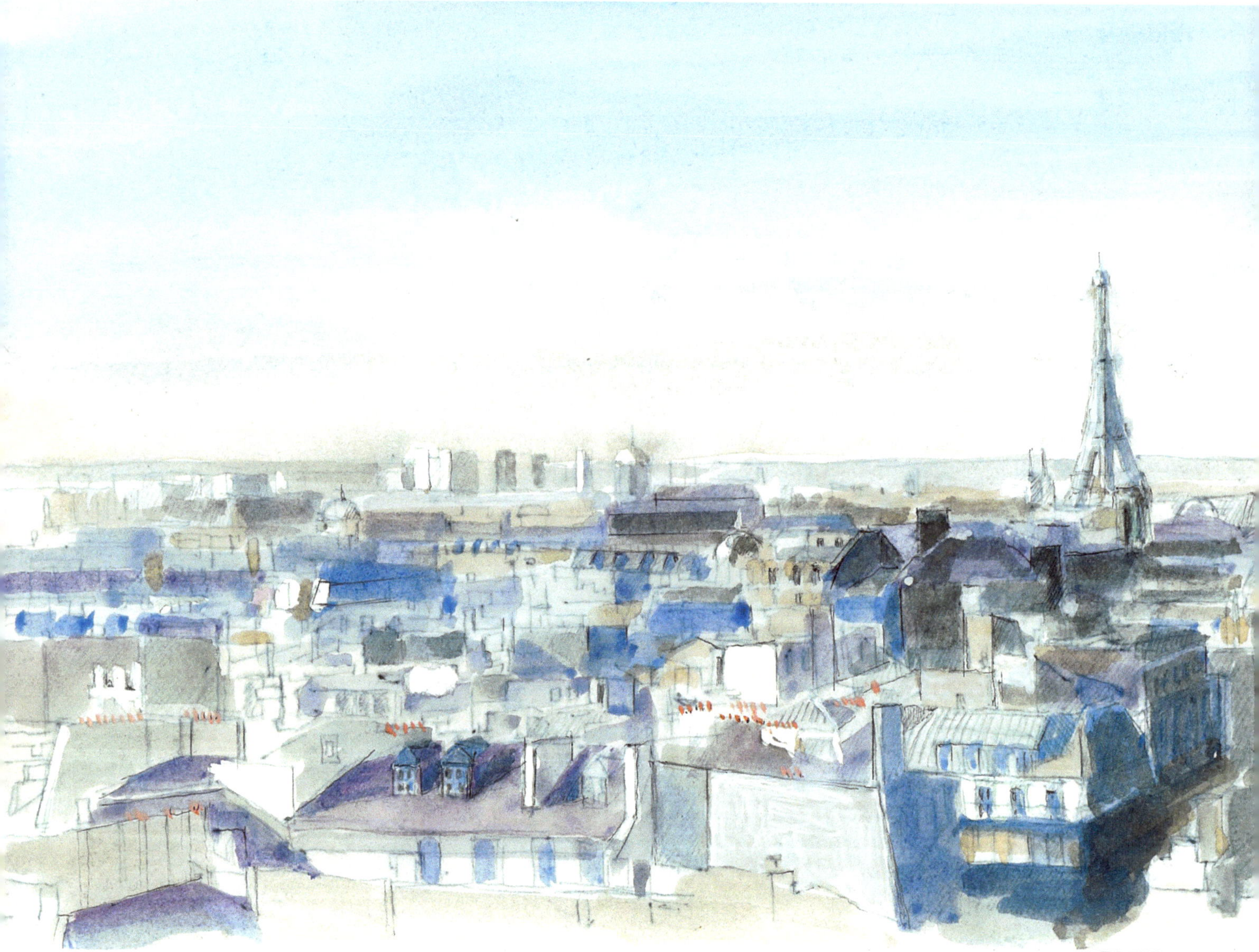

EUSTACHE DESCHAMPS, 1370

She is the city crowned above the rest,
the fount of scholarship and wisdom, and its well,
located on the river Seine, possessed
of woods and vineyards, land and dell.
She has more of the mortal good that we embrace
than any other place;
all strangers love her, will always find her fair,
because such elegance, such happiness,
will not be found in any town but this:
Paris is beyond compare.

Index of Illustrations

THE LEFT BANK

THE RIVER SEINE AND THE ISLANDS CITÉ AND SAINT-LOUIS

THE RIGHT BANK

Index of quotes and copyright acknowledgements

www.ingramcontent.com/pod-product-compliance
Ingram Content Group UK Ltd.
Pitfield, Milton Keynes, MK11 3LW, UK
UKHW060101300726
14090UKWH00003B/338

* 9 7 8 2 7 4 6 6 8 4 2 1 8 *